Herman Barnes
From
Aunt Rebecca.

Christmas
1893.

A NEW ENGLAND BOYHOOD.

"GOVERNOR LINCOLN WALKED UP WINTER STREET WITHOUT ANY CADETS."—*Page* 108.

A NEW
ENGLAND
BOYHOOD

BY

EDWARD E. HALE

AUTHOR OF "EAST AND WEST," "SYBIL KNOX," "HOW
THEY LIVED AT HAMPTON," ETC., ETC.

NEW YORK
CASSELL PUBLISHING COMPANY
104 & 106 FOURTH AVENUE

INTRODUCTION.

A CHARMING writer, Miss Lucy Larcom, published a few years ago a charming book called "A New England Girlhood." She described in it her own early life, first in Beverly, opposite Salem on the seashore of Massachusetts, with its gardens and beaches and fishing boats; then in Lowell in its infant days, with its river and waterfalls and Arcadian cotton factories.

Mr. Horace Scudder, editor of the *Atlantic Monthly*, was as much attracted by this pleasant book as the rest of us. It suggested to him the possibility of another book, which should deal with the same years, now becoming mythical, as a New England boy saw life in the little New England city of those days—the only city of New England which took that name before 1826, excepting the city of Vergennes in Vermont and that of Hartford in Connecticut.

Quite leaving Hartford out, in my earliest days it was always a joke at home, if anyone spoke of Boston as the only city, for some one to say, "Boston and Vergennes." Vergennes was incorporated in 1788, by the legislature of Vermont, which was then an independent nation, not belonging either to the Confederacy of the United States or sharing in the deliberations for the new constitution.

Mr. Scudder asked me to furnish some chapters, with the attractive title of "A New England Boyhood," from my own memories, in such form that they might be published in the *Atlantic Monthly*. And this I was glad to do. Those chapters, published in that magazine in 1892, make more than half of the book now in the reader's hands.

I have to say this by way of introduction, because here is my only excuse for what else seems the conceit of introducing little bits of personal experience into my story, of no earthly value to anybody but myself and my children, excepting as they illustrate the simplicity and ease of a phase of New England life, which has now wholly passed away. I do not flatter myself that I have succeeded in presenting to the reader the simplicity and the dignity of that life, so curiously combined as simplicity and dignity were. Those people, in the little seaport of Boston, lived and moved as if they were people of the most important city of the world. What is more, they meant to make Boston the purest, noblest, and best city in the world. And they lived there in some forms of social life which would have become princes of sixty-four quarterings, with some which were identical with those of the log-cabin. Every man of them was an American, and believed to the sole of his feet that there was no fit government for men but that of a republic. All the same, their leaders, men and women, were dignified, elegant, and gracious in their bearing and manner; and there was no prince in the world who better understood the bearing and the customs of gentlemen and gentlewomen.

It was a good place in which to be born, and a good place in which to grow to manhood.

From 1630, when Boston was founded by an important branch of Winthrop's colony, to 1826, when these reminiscences begin, it had grown, slowly and not very regularly, from a little hamlet of settlers, sick and half starved, to a brisk commercial town of about forty-five thousand people. There is no better description than Mr. Emerson's, which I heard him read, fresh from his own notes, on the platform of Faneuil Hall, on the centennial of the Boston Tea-Party, December 16, 1873. It was said that he had written the last verses in the train as he rode from Concord. The notes in his hand were on various bits of paper, and I believe that the poem was born on that day.

> The rocky nook, with hill-tops three,
>   Looked eastward from the farms,
> And twice each day the flowing sea
>   Took Boston in its arms.
>
> .   .   .   .   .
>
> The wild rose and the barberry thorn
>   Hung out their summer pride,
> Where now on heated pavements worn
>   The feet of millions stride.

Fair rose the planted hills behind
   The good town on the bay,
And where the western hills declined
   The prairie stretched away.

.   .   .   .   .

Each street leads downward to the sea,
   Or landward to the west.

The first certain description of the place is that in Bradford : " We came into the bottom of the bay ; but being late we anchored and lay in the shallop, not having seen any of the people. The next morning we put in for the shore. There we found many lobsters that had been gathered together."

This camping ground is Copp's Hill at the very northern end of the peninsula. The lobsters were taken near the landing of the ferry, which afterward took men to Charlestown. If Tom, Dick, and Harry had been left to their own devices, if no paternal or fraternal government had protected their industries and done better for them than nature did, if successive generations had been left to do what nature bade, as is now the theory of the "let alones," making head again in the midst

of our matchless prosperity—a few hundred of
us, who had survived in the struggle for existence, would be trapping lobsters at the North
End to-day. Where the other hundred thousand people would be, who now inhabit the old
peninsula, I do not know—or, indeed, if they
would have been at all.

A peninsula it was ; but no geographer in
his senses would give that name now to the
bulging cape which has expanded on either
side of the old almost island. At high tides,
in gales, the water washed across what was
then called the Neck, and is still called so by
old-fashioned people. Three hills, of which
the highest was 138 feet high from the sea,
broke the surface of the peninsula, and of
these the top of the highest was broken again
by three smaller hills. This highest hill is
Beacon Hill. Copp's Hill was at the north,
and Fort Hill on the east. For the convenience of trade Fort Hill has been entirely
removed, and a little circular bit of greensward
marks the place where, in my boyhood, was a
hill fifty feet high.

In old days a canal was cut across the town,

separating the Copp's Hill elevation from those south of it. A tidal mill was arranged here, by retaining the water at high tide in the mill-pond, and letting it dribble out when the tide had fallen. The average rise and fall of the tide in Boston is about ten feet, so that this contrivance gave power enough for grinding corn when there was corn to grind. The mill-pond was filled up about the period to which the reminiscences in this book belong.

If this book should stray into the hands of persons who do not know the physical Boston of to-day, or the physical Boston of history, it may be worth while, "for the greater caution," as the lawyers say, to give an outline map of both. In the sketch in the margin the white nucleus represents the Boston which Bradford found, and where we should have been catching lobsters had there been no paternal government or other government, until to-day. The outline of the larger cape, as I have called it, is the outline of Boston now, when what we called the "flats" have been filled in by successive improvements—if improvements they are. Any person, who desires to know my

North

OLD BOSTON AND NEW

opinion on such improvements, may consult the study I have made on similar subjects in my book called "Sybaris." I am, however, an optimist, and after a thing has been done I accept it. I dictate these words as I lie on my back on a comfortable sofa in a comfortable room in the vestry of the church which stands where, in boyhood, I could have skated, or could have caught smelts for the next day's breakfast. For the temperature outside, at this moment, is ten degrees above zero, a temperature which was very favorable for the catching of smelts in those days.

Politically or socially, the period between 1820 and 1835 belongs to the period when Boston was turning to internal commerce and the development of manufacture, and was relinquishing that maritime commerce which had created her. The Southern and Western leaders of the country, not disinclined to thwart the maritime industries of New England, had attempted to build up what Mr. Clay called "the American system" of home manufacture. So soon as this system established itself, the New Englanders adapted themselves to the new conditions, and set up their manufactories on the borders of their streams— Pawtucket, Waltham, Lowell, and, afterwards, Manchester, Lawrence, and Holyoke came into being. The necessity of closer communication with the interior was as distinctly felt in New England as in the Middle States. The Middlesex Canal, an elaborate system of turnpikes, and, later yet, the present system of railroads were established. But in the year 1830 Boston still retained a large East Indian and European commerce. It is interesting to see how largely the exports were still products of the forests and the fisheries.

And, not to smirch the pages of this little book with any of the ashes of theological controversy which is long since dead, it may be mentioned that, in the years between 1820 and 1840, Boston was the centre of theological discussion, which undoubtedly greatly quickened the religious life of New England. In those years there was a certain expectation of a speedy improvement, not to say revolution, in social order, such as men do not often experience. Dr. Channing was preaching the gospel of the divinity of man. Dr. Tuckerman, Frederick Gray, Charles Barnard and Robert Cassie Waterston, with others, were introducing practical illustrations of improvement. There was plenty of money, and the rich men of Boston really meant that here should be a model and ideal city. The country was prosperous; they were prosperous, and they looked forward to a noble future.

At the same time they had the advantage of having a university close under their lee, which they were themselves managing. They had started their Athenæum, with the collections of pictures and statues, and a good library. They had a good deal of leisure; and a certain interest, not wholly the interest of dilettanti, in fine arts and literature, gave distinction to the little town.

Into such a community it was my good fortune to be born, on the morning of the 3d of April, 1822.

I do not attempt anything so ambitious as an autobiography. But a man sees with his own eyes, and a boy even more than a man; and what I remember of a New England boyhood is what mine was, not what anyone else lived through in the same time. There will be a certain convenience, then, to the reader if he knows a little of the household and family in which the boyhood was spent which in these chapters is described.

In the ship *Lion*, in the voyage of Winthrop's fleet, came to Boston Robert Hale, who was, I suppose, of the Hales of Kent. Searching in the wills of that time in Canterbury, in Kent, I found this:

7. "To my sonne John Hales, five pounds and my best silver guilt sword, yet nevertheless and on this condition"—that he do not intercept the execution of the rest of the will.

And I have a fancy that that son was cut off with a "guilt sword" because he was a Puritan, while the rest of the Hales, or Haleses, were very High Church. So High Church have they been in later times that it was one of them, Sir James Hales, who accompanied James II. into exile. Somehow I connect him with the throwing the Great Seal into the Thames. Within my own memory Hales

Place, near Canterbury, has become the seat of a Jesuit school for the training of priests.

This Robert Hale is called a blacksmith, and he settled at Charlestown, opposite Boston. He seems to have had the taste for surveying or engineering which crops out in alternate generations in the family. He was of the party which was sent to Winnipiseogee to run the northern line of Massachusetts. The stone which they set there is to be seen to this day. He married Joanna Cutter. He sent his son John Hale to Harvard College, where he was the fourth in social rank of his class of eight. He became the minister of Beverly, is the John Hale who went to Quebec as chaplain and was taken prisoner, and the John Hale of the Salem witchcraft. A missal given him by a Catholic priest in Quebec is in the library of Harvard College to this day. He was the grandfather, by his oldest son, of King Hale, as Robert Hale (H. C., 1686) was familiarly called in Beverly ; and by his fourth son, Samuel, was grandfather of my father's grandfather, Richard Hale, who lived in Coventry, Conn., and died in 1802. This Richard Hale was father of Captain Nathan Hale of the Revolutionary history, and of Enoch Hale, my grandfather, alluded to in chapter vii. of this book.

In 1636 Richard Everett, or Everard, appears in Watertown, and afterwards in Springfield and Dedham. In Dedham he died. From him came a line of farmers, who are called captain, deacon, and so on till we come to Ebenezer Everett of Tiot, now called Norwood, a village of South Dedham. He was father of Rev. Oliver Everett (H. C., 1772), who was minister of the New South Church in Boston, and was my grandfather on my mother's side.

For my father, Nathan Hale, oldest son of Rev. Enoch Hale above, on a day to be marked with vermilion with me and mine, namely, September 5, 1816, married Sarah Preston Everett, my mother, daughter of Rev. Oliver Everett. On that day she was twenty years old ; he was thirty-two.

It is pity of pities that we never made him write "A New England Boyhood" as he saw it. For he was born in 1784, the year after the peace with England. He grew up in the very purest conditions of the simplest and, indeed, the best life of New England. His father had been for eight years the minister of a frontier town, Westhampton, in the days when the minister was chosen by the town in open town meeting, was paid by the town, and regarded himself as personally responsible for the moral and spiritual life of everybody in the town.

Hoeing corn or potatoes one day in the summer of 1800, my father, a boy of sixteen, was called into his father's study, where he found Dr. Fitch, then the president of Williams College, which had been established as a college seven years before. Dr. Fitch had stopped in a journey across country, to accept the hospitalities of the parsonage. The boy was told to show Dr. Fitch how well he could read Latin ; then he read to him from the Greek Testament, and Dr. Fitch said he was ready to enter Williams College. His father and he had not expected that he would enter until the next year. But this fortunate visit of the president carried him to Williamstown that summer, and he graduated there in the class of 1804.

He and the other boys from that region used to ride across Berkshire County on horseback when the college terms began. A younger boy drove the horses back in a drove, and, when vacation came, took them to the college again for the students to ride back upon. A part of the road was a turnpike where tolls were collected. When they approached the gate they would all dismount, and on foot drive the horses in front of them, and demand the right of passing at the rate for a drove of horses or cattle. Nothing, as they said, was said about saddles or bridles. When I asked once if the toll-keeper submitted meekly to this, I was told that they generally had to pay the full toll, but that the tollman expected to treat them to cider all round.

The college was divided into two societies— the Philomathian and the Philotechnian. I think the latter exists in Williamstown in some form still. I have seen the records of debates: "Question, Whether the purchase of

Louisiana is desirable.   Decided in the nega-
tive, 17 to 1.'' For they were high and hot
Federalists.

I have my father's part when he graduated.
It is on the improvements in social order
made in the last fifty years.

So soon as he left college he engaged as
tutor in the family of John J. Dickinson in
Troy, not far from Williamstown.   But he
went home first, and on his way to Troy went
to the city of New York for the first time.
The population was only about seventy-five
thousand.   It was three years before Fulton's
Clermont, his first steamboat, went up the
Hudson, and the tradition in our family is
that my father went up the river in a sloop to
Troy, was a fortnight in going, and read
through Gibbon's "Decline and Fall" on
the way.

Judging from his accomplishments Williams College must have done its work well.
He read Latin well and with pleasure to the
end of his life.   He did not keep up his Greek
with the same interest, but he was an accurate
Greek scholar.   He was a mathematician of

high rank in the mathematics of those days, and was afterward quite the peer in those lines of the engineers with whom he worked on the great public works of which he had the charge. He studied some Hebrew in college, and could always read a little. I asked him once if this was with any thought of being a minister, but he said, "No, but there was nothing else to study." He had to learn his French and German afterward, and did. I think that in my boyhood there were more German books in our house than perhaps in any other house in Boston. But that is saying very little; as late as 1843 I could buy no German books, even in Pennsylvania, but Goethe and Schiller and the Lutheran hymn-book.

After a year in Troy he received the appointment of preceptor in mathematics in Exeter Academy in New Hampshire. He crossed Massachusetts to Boston on his way to Exeter. Here is a memorandum of the way in which this was done:

The arrangement of the stages was that if the stages coming from Springfield and Northampton had more

passengers than could go on one stage some of them had
to stop ; and those who got on last were the ones who
had to stop.

I arrived at Brookfield at night, having left Northampton in the morning.   The person who had come the
shortest distance was a lady.   She was in great distress
that she could not go on.   I had a sort of desire to stay
there to see Howe and Henshaw, but I should not have
thought of staying a day but to let this lady go on.

At Exeter, in the charming society of that
place, he met the Peabodys and Alexander
Hill Everett, who was the other "preceptor,"
the preceptor of Greek and Latin.   He graduated at Harvard in 1806.   These two young
men became very fond of each other, and when,
in 1808 my father determined to leave Exeter
and come to Boston to study law, he became
acquainted with all Mr. Everett's Boston
friends.

Meanwhile, when he was twelve years old,
my mother had been born, in Dorchester, now
a part of the municipality of Boston.   Her
father, in delicate health, had left his charge
in 1792.   Her mother was a Boston girl, one of
the daughters of Alexander Sears Hill and
Mary Richey of Santa Cruz.   The tradition
was that Alexander Sears Hill had gone to

Philadelphia for a milder climate in winter, had fallen in love with Mary Richey, and that they had married without the knowledge of their parents. A handsome couple they were, as the full-length portraits by Copley attest to this day. They both died young. I have the love-letters which passed between Lucy Hill and Oliver Everett; it was a happy marriage until his death, but he died in consumption in 1802. After this the family lived sometimes in the North End of Boston, sometimes in the old house in Dorchester. In 1812 Edward Everett, the third son, was ordained minister of Brattle Street Church in Boston. He was not married—was, indeed, but twenty years old. His mother and sister moved into the parsonage in Court Street, where are now the offices of Adams Express. Mr. Everett left that church in the year 1815, and my grandmother and her family established themselves in a house in Bumstead Place—a place which exists no longer—and there my mother was married.

The newly married couple lived first in Ashburton Place, then called Somerset Court, in a house now standing. A year or two after they removed to Tremont Street to a house which has been absorbed by Parker's Hotel, the second from where the Tremont Theatre was built in 1827. Here I was born. The family afterwards lived at the corner of School Street in a house which also has been absorbed by Parker's. In 1828 we removed to No. 1 Tremont Place, a house still standing; and in 1833 to one of Mr. Andrews's houses in Central Court, a property now covered by Jordan & Marsh's, just behind where old Judge Sewall lived most of his life. It is in the four houses last named that the scenery of the home life described in these chapters is to be placed.

CONTENTS.

A NEW ENGLAND BOYHOOD.

CHAPTER I.

'TIS SEVENTY YEARS SINCE.

THE reader and I ought not to begin without my reminding him that the Boston of which I am to write was very different from the Boston of to-day. In 1825 Boston was still a large country town. I think some one has called it a city of gardens; but that some one may have been I. As late as 1817, in a description of Boston which accompanied a show which a Frenchman had made by carving and painting the separate houses, it was said, with some triumph, that there were nine blocks of buildings in the town. This means that all the other buildings stood with windows or doors on each of the four sides, and in most instances with trees, or perhaps little lanes, between; as all people will live when the Kingdom of

Heaven comes. To people in this neighborhood to-day, I may say that the upper part of
the main street in Charlestown gives a very
good idea of what the whole of Washington
Street south of Winter Street was then.   And,
by the way, Washington Street was much
more often called Main Street than by its
longer name.

The reader must imagine, therefore, a large,
pretty country town, where stage-coaches still
clattered in from the country, and brought all
the strangers who did not ride in their own
chaises.   Large stables, always of wood, I
think, provided for the horses thus needed.   I
remember, as I write, Niles's stable in School
Street, a large stable in Bromfield Street, afterward Streeter's, the stables of the Marlborough Hotel in Washington Street, and what
seemed to us very large stables in Hawley
Street—all in the very heart of the town, and
on a tract which cannot be more than twelve
acres.   When, in 1829, it was reported that the
new Tremont House was to have no special
stables for its guests, the announcement
excited surprise almost universal ; and to us

children the statement that there was to be a tavern, or a hotel, without a sign, was still more extraordinary. We were used to seeing swinging signs on posts in front of the taverns. Thus I remember "The Indian Queen" in Bromfield Street, "The Bunch of Grapes" in State Street, "The Lamb" I think where the Adams House now is, "The Lion" where the Boston Theatre is, and nearly opposite these the Lafayette Tavern. This means that large pictures of an Indian queen, a bunch of grapes, a lamb, a lion, and of Lafayette swung backward and forward in the wind. There was a sign in front of the Marlborough Tavern, and one nearly opposite, south of Milk Street, but I do not remember what these were. All these inns would now be thought small. They were then called taverns, and to New Englanders seemed very large. Of course they were large enough for their purpose. When I was nine or ten years old my father, who was thought to be a fanatic as a railroad prophet, offered in Faneuil Hall the suggestion that if people could come from Springfield to Boston in five hours an average of nine people would come every day. This prophecy was then considered extravagant. I have told the story, in the Introduction, of his coming to Boston for the first time, in 1805, when the Northampton passengers joined the Springfield passengers at Brookfield. There was room in the carriage for six only. He therefore gave up his seat to a lady who had pressing duties, and waited in Brookfield twenty-four hours to take his chances for the next stage.

The more important business streets of this town of Boston were paved in the middle with round stones from the neighboring beaches, then as now called cobble-stones—I do not know why; but an accomplished friend, who reads this in manuscript, says that the lapstone on which a cobbler stretches his leather is a cobble-stone. I recommend this etymology to Dr. Murray and Dr. Whitney. The use of bricks for sidewalks was just coming in, but generally the sidewalks were laid with flat slates or shales from the neighborhood, which were put down in any shape they happened to take in splitting, without being squared at the corners. Bromfield Street, Winter Street,

Summer Street, and Washington Street (old Marlborough Street) between School and Winter seem to us now to be narrow streets, but they have all been widened considerably within my memory. Bromfield Street was called Bromfield's Lane.

On the other hand, so far as I remember the houses themselves and the life in them, everything was quite as elegant and finished as it is now. Furniture was stately, solid, and expensive. I use chairs, tables, and a sideboard in my house to-day, which are exactly as good now as they were then. Carpets, then of English make, covered the whole floor, and were of what we should now call perfect quality. In summer, by the way, in all houses of which I knew anything, these carpets were always taken up, and India mattings substituted in the "living-rooms." Observe that very few houses were closed in summer. Dress was certainly as elegant and costly as it is now ; so were porcelain, glass, table linen, and all table furniture. In the earlier days of which I write, a decanter of wine would invariably have stood on a sideboard in every parlor, so that a glass

of wine could readily be offered at any moment
to any guest.   All through my boyhood it
would have been matter of remark if, when
a visitor made an evening call, something to
eat or drink was not produced at nine o'clock.
It might be crackers and cheese, it might be
mince pie, it might be oysters or cold chicken.
But something would appear as certainly as
there would be a fire on the hearth in winter.
Every house, by the way, was warmed by open
fires ; and in every kitchen cooking was done
by an open fire.   I doubt if I ever saw a stove
in my boyhood except in a school or an office.
Anthracite coal was first tried in Boston in
1824.   Gas appeared about the same time.   I
was taken, as a little boy, to see it burning
in the shops in Washington Street, and to
wonder at an elephant, a tortoise, and a cow,
which spouted burning gas in one window.
Gas was not introduced into dwelling-houses
until Pemberton Square was built by the
Lowells, Jacksons, and their friends, in the
years 1835, 1836, and later.   It was a surprise
to everyone when Papanti introduced it in
his new Papanti's Hall.   To prepare for that

occasion the ground-glass shades had a little rouge shaken about in the interior, that the white gaslight might not be too unfavorable to the complexion of the beauties below. Whether this device is still thought necessary in ballrooms I do not know; but I suggest it as a hint to the wise.

A handsome parlor then, differed from a handsome parlor now, mostly in the minor matters of decoration. The pictures on the walls were few, and were mostly portraits. For the rest, mirrors were large and handsome. You would see some copies from well-known paintings in European galleries, and any one who had an Allston would be glad to show it. But I mean that most walls were bare. In good houses, if modern, the walls of parlors would invariably be painted of one neutral tint; but in older houses there would be paper hangings, perhaps of landscape patterns. The furniture of a parlor would generally be twelve decorous heavy chairs, probably hair-seated, with their backs against the walls; a sofa which matched them, also with its back against the wall; and a heavy,

perhaps marble-topped centre table. There
might be a rocking-chair in the room also ;
but, so far as I remember, other easy-chairs,
scattered as one chose about a room, were
unknown.

Try to recall, dear reader, or to imagine,
the conditions of a town without any railroads, and without any steam navigation
beyond fifteen miles. The first steamboat in
Boston harbor went to Nahant and back
again, about 1826. The first steam railway
ran trains to Newton, nine miles, in 1833.
Please to remember, then, that everybody
lived in Boston the year round, excepting a
handful of rich people who had country
places in Dorchester, Roxbury, Newton,
Brookline, Watertown, Waltham, Brighton,
Cambridge, Charlestown, or Medford, accessible by a horse and chaise. What we call
buggies were unknown, and a gentleman and
lady would certainly ride in a chaise, which
was not the English chaise, but a two-wheeled
covered vehicle, hung on C-springs. In such
a town the supplies of food, unless brought
from the immediate neighborhood, came from

the seaboard or the Western rivers in sloops
or schooners. We drew our flour from points
as far south as Richmond. I remember that,
in more than one winter, when my grandmother, in Westhampton, had sent us a keg
or two of home apple-sauce, the sloop which
brought the treasure was frozen up in Connecticut River below Hartford, so that it was
four or five months before we hungry children
enjoyed her present. Great wagons with
large teams of horses brought from the interior such products as did not come in this
way.

For these horses and wagons there were,
on "the Neck" and beyond, great sheds
and stables. The country teamster left his
horses and his load there while he came
into town to make sure where it was to be
delivered. To pick up the stray corn which
was scattered in these sheds great flocks of
pigeons congregated, of whom a wretched
handful survive to this day. I mention these
little details to give some idea of the country
fashion of our lives. Two or three weeks out
of town in summer was a large allowance

of vacation. Nobody dreamed of closing a church in summer. The school vacation was a fortnight and three days in August, to which, in later days, was added first one week, and then two weeks in June. The summer break-up which now divides everybody's Boston year was then wholly unknown.

CHAPTER II.

SCHOOL LIFE.

AFTER studying with great care Mr. Howell's "Boy's Town" and Miss Larcom's "New England Girlhood," I have determined not to follow a strict order of time. For better, for worse, I will throw in together in one chapter a set of school memories which range from about 1825 for ten years. At my own imprudent request, not to say urgency, I was sent to school with two sisters and a brother, older than I, when I was reckoned as about two years old. The school was in an old-fashioned wooden house which fronted on a little yard entered from Summer Street. We went up one flight of narrow stairs, and here the northern room of the two bedrooms of the house was occupied by Miss Susan Whitney for her school, and the southern room, which had windows on

11

Summer Street, by Miss Ayres, of whom Miss Whitney had formerly been an assistant. Miss Whitney afterwards educated more than one generation of the children of Boston families. I supposed her to be one of the most aged, and certainly the most learned, women of her time. I believe she was a kind-hearted, intelligent girl of seventeen, when I first knew her. I also supposed the room to be a large hall, though I knew it was not nearly so large as our own parlors at home. It may have been eighteen feet square. The floor was sanded with clean sand every Thursday and Saturday afternoon. This was a matter of practical importance to us, because with the sand, using our feet as tools, we made sand pies. You gather the sand with the inside edge of either shoe from a greater or less distance, as the size of the pie requires. As you gain skill, the heap which you make is more and more round. When it is well rounded you flatten it by a careful pressure of one foot from above. Hence it will be seen that full success depends on your keeping the sole of the shoe exactly parallel with the

plane of the floor. If you find you have succeeded when you withdraw the shoe, you
prick the pie with a pin or a broom splint provided for the purpose, pricking it in whatever
pattern you like. The skill of a good pie-
maker is measured largely by these patterns.
It will readily be seen that the pie is better if
the sand is a little moist. But beggars cannot
be choosers, and while we preferred the sand
on Mondays and Fridays, when it was fresh,
we took it as it came.

I dwell on this detail at length because it is
one instance as good as a hundred of the way
in which we adapted ourselves to the conditions of our times. Children now have carpets on their kindergarten floors, where sand
is unknown; so we have to provide clay for
them to model with, and put a heap of sand
in the back yard. Miss Whitney provided for
the same needs by a simpler device, which I
dare say is as old as King Alfred.

I cannot tell how we were taught to read,
for I cannot remember the time when I could
not read as well as I can now. There was a
little spelling-book called "The New York

Spelling-Book," printed by Mahlon Day. When, afterwards, I came to read about Mahlon in the book of Ruth, my notion of him was of a man who had the same name as the man who published the spelling-book. My grandfather had made a spelling-book which we had at home. Privately, I knew that, because he made it, it must be better than the book at school, but I was far too proud to explain this to Miss Whitney. I accepted her spelling-book in the same spirit in which I have often acted since, falling in with what I saw was the general drift, because the matter was of no great consequence. For reading-books we had Mrs. Barbauld's "First Lessons," "Come hither, Charles, come to mamma"; and we had "Popular Lessons," by Miss Robbins, which would be a good book to revive now, but I have not seen it for sixty years.

The school must have been a very much "go-as-you-please" sort of place. So far it conformed to the highest ideals of the best modern systems. But it had rewards and punishments. I have now a life of William Tell which was given me as a prize when I was five years old. By way of showing what was then thought fit reading for boys of that age I copy the first sentence: "Friends of liberty, magnanimous hearts, sons of sensibility, ye who know how to die for your independence and live only for your brethren, lend an ear to my accents. Come! hear how one single man, born in an uncivilized clime, in the midst of a people curbed beneath the rods of an oppressor, by his individual courage, raised this people so abased, and gave it a new being"—and so on, and so on. My brother Nathan had "Rasselas" for a prize, and my sister Sarah had a silver medal, "To the most amiable," which I am sure she deserved, though the competition extended to the whole world.

But these were the great prizes. In an old desk, of which the cover had been torn off, in the closet at the left of the fireplace, were a number of bows made of yellow, pink, and blue ribbon. When Saturday came, every child "who had been good" during the week was permitted to select one of these bows, choosing his own color, and to have it pinned

on his clothes under his chin to wear home.
If, on the other hand, he had been very bad, he
had a black bow affixed, willy nilly. I hardly
dare to soil this page with the tale, but there
was an awful story that a boy, whom I will
call Charles Waters, unpinned his black bow
and trod it in the dirt of the street. But I
hasten to add, that in that innocent community no one believed this dreadful story.
Indeed, it was whispered from one to another,
rather as an index of what terrible stories
were afloat in the world than with any feeling
that it could possibly be true.

It is certainly a little queer that in after
years one remembers such trifles as this, and
forgets absolutely the weightier matters of the
law ; how he learned to read and write ; how
he fought with the angel of vulgar fractions
and compelled him to grant a blessing ; how,
in a word, one learned anything of importance.
But so it is ; and thus, as I have said, I have no
memory of any time when I could not read as
well as I can now. Perhaps that is the reason
why I am too apt to rank teachers of elocution
with dancing-masters and fencing-masters, and

"I WAS READING A BOOK WITH PERFECT SATISFACTION."
—*Page* 17.

other professors of deportment. Dear Miss Whitney must have taught us well, or we should have remembered the process more sadly.

If this is a book of confessions I ought to tell my crimes, and one sin I certainly committed at Miss Whitney's school. But alas, I do not know what it was, and I never did. Only this I know. We were all too small to go home through Main Street alone. Fullum came for us at twelve, and again at five in the afternoon. Who Fullum was shall appear by and by. One day, when Fullum came at noon, he found me seated in a large yellow chair in the middle of the school-room. I was reading a book with perfect satisfaction. So soon as Fullum appeared, I was lifted from the chair and my "things" were put on. When we were in the street Fullum said, "What have you been doing that was naughty, doctor?" I told him, with perfect sincerity, that I had done nothing wrong. But this he did not believe. He reminded me of what I then recollected, that that yellow chair was always a seat of punishment. I had certainly never seen

any one in it before—unless it were Miss Whitney herself — excepting the sinners of the
school, placed there for punishment. But alas,
it had not occurred to any one to tell me why
I was put there ; and as my own conscience
was clear, I have not known from that day to
this what my offence was.

I could probably without much difficulty
make a volume on Miss Whitney's school, and
the various aspects of life as they there presented themselves to me. But these papers
must be severely condensed, and I omit such
details. To me personally they have a little
value, as bearing on the question how far back
our memory really runs. There is a Frenchman who says that he recollects the relief produced on his eyes when he was a baby, thirty-
six hours old, and a nurse lowered a curtain to
screen him from the light. I am not able to
fix any facts as early as this ; but I am interested in the observation that, among these
early recollections of Miss Whitney, there is
not included the slightest memory of my first
interviews with her. I had a brother and two
sisters older than myself, who were my home

playmates. I saw them go to school from day to day, and I finally cried because I wanted to go with them. Miss Whitney was therefore persuaded to receive a pupil two years old at the school. It speaks well for her, I think, that she found it possible to adapt such a young gentleman to the exercises of the academy.

This makes me think, as I have said, that those exercises must have been conducted on the individual plan. But my chief memories of the school are of conducting observations, similar to Tyndall's, on the effect produced by sunlight upon dust floating in the air. Such luxuries as window-shades or blinds were unknown; if the sun shone in on the south side of the room you shut an inside shutter. This reminds me that inside shutters are almost wholly unknown to the rising generation, but then every house of which I knew anything had them. At the top of this shutter, which was of panelled wood, a heart was cut, so as to let a little light into the room when the shutters were closed. It will readily be seen that this heart made very curious forms on the floating dust in the school-room. What with the manufacture of sand pies and other enterprises going on, there must have been a good deal of dust in the school-room, and I remember far better the aspects of this dust, as the sun lighted it and as it floated in different currents, than I do any single lesson which I acquired from books.

It will give some idea of the simplicity of manners and of the quietness of the little town if I tell how " we four "—by which I mean the four oldest children of my father's family— went to school and returned, in the winter.

In winter Fullum put my two sisters, my brother, and myself into a little green sleigh which he had had made, in which he dragged us over the snow to school. I believe that if any Fullum of to-day should start from the upper door of the Parker House, and drag four little children down School Street, through Washington Street, to Summer Street, and stop at a door opposite Hovey's, he would attract a fair share of attention. But there was room enough for all then. The " main street " was what the chief street of a good

country town would be now, and this equipage
seemed strange to nobody.

School kept only in the morning on Saturday, and Thursday afternoon was always a holiday, in memory of the "Thursday lecture." *
But as the lecture was delivered at eleven
o'clock in the morning, and every school kept
until twelve, there was, of course, no real connection between the holiday and the lecture.
The half-holiday was changed to Wednesday,
a few years later than the time I am speaking
of. It is on this account that Wednesday and
Saturday appear to me, to this moment, the
happiest days of the week. For I may as well
say, first as last, that school was always a bore

---

* The Thursday lecture was a regular function, in which
one of the Congregational ministers of Boston addressed such
audiences as came together on Thursday. At this time the
congregation consisted simply of the ministers of the town
and neighborhood, and such ladies, generally past youth, as
liked to go to hear the city clerk read the intentions of marriage. The law then required that these intentions should be
read three times before some public assembly, and the Thursday lecture was dignified by the name of a public assembly.
But in older times the lecture had been much more important.
To tell the whole truth, the restrictions in England, on such
week-day addresses as were made by distinguished preachers,
drove the particular thorn in the side of the Puritan which did

to me. I did not so much hate it, as dislike
it, as a necessary nuisance. I think all my
teachers regarded it as such ; I am sure they
made me so regard it.

Just before I was six years old I was transferred from Miss Whitney's school to another
school which was in the immediate neighborhood, being in the basement of the First
Church, which was then in Chauncy Street.
It stood, I think, just where Coleman & Mead's
great store is to-day. There were three or four
large rooms under the church, which were
rented as school-rooms ; and it being thought
that I was large enough to go to a man's

most to drive him to his new home in the West. Cotton and
the other preachers had all been imprisoned, or threatened
with being imprisoned, because they would deliver these
week-day lectures. The people who emigrated were absolutely determined that they would hear them, and that is probably the reason why the reader and I are in this country—
because our ancestors chose to go to church in the middle of
the week. When they came here they established the Thursday lecture. Cotton's fame and eloquence were such that the
Thursday lecture gave Boston its pre-eminence in the Bay, a
pre-eminence which it did not have before Cotton arrived. So
that the Thursday lecture has a definite historical interest to a
Boston born man. But the average Boston man long since
ceased to go to hear it, and it is now discontinued.

school, I was sent there, to my great delight, with my friend Edward Webster. We were very intimate from days earlier than this, of which I will speak in another chapter, and it was a great pleasure to us that we could go to school together. He had been at Miss Ayres's, so that only an entry parted us. There was no thought of sending me to a public school.

My father and mother had both very decided, and, I have a right to say, very advanced, views on matters of education ; and advanced education was then a matter everywhere in the air. The Boston Latin School had been made a first-rate school for preparing boys for college, under the eye and care of Benjamin Apthorp Gould, some ten years before. But there was no public school of any lower grade, to which my father would have sent me, any more than he would have sent me to jail. Since that time I have heard my contemporaries talk of the common school training of the day, and I do not wonder at my father's decision. The masters, so far as I know, were all inferior men ; there was constant talk of "hiding" and "cow-hides" and

"ferules" and "thrashing," and I should say,
indeed, that the only recollections of my contemporaries about those school-days are of one
constant low conflict with men of a very low
type. So soon as a boy was sent to the Latin
School—and he was sent there at nine years of
age—all this was changed into the life of a
civilized place. Why the Boston people toler-
ated such brutality as went on in their other
public schools I do not know, and never have
known; but no change came for some years
after.

For the next three years the only object, so
far as I was concerned, was to have me live
along and get ready for the Latin School. I
have always been glad that I was sent where I
was—to a school without any plan or machinery, very much on the go-as-you-please principle, and where there was no strain put upon
the pupil. I disliked it, as I disliked all
schools; but here, again, I regarded the whole
arrangement as one of those necessary nui-
sances which society imposes on the individual,
and which the individual would be foolish if he
quarrelled with, when he did not have it in his

power to abolish it. I had no such power, and therefore went and came as I was bidden, only eager every day to exchange the monotonies of school life for the more varied and larger enterprises of the play-room or of the Common.

I have said that advanced education was in the air. It will be hard to make boys and girls of the present day understand how much was then expected from reforms in education. Dr. Channing was at his best then, and all that he had to say about culture and self-culture impressed people intensely—more intensely, I think, than was good for them. There were rumors from Europe of Fellenberg's school at Hofwyl. At Northampton the Round Hill School was started in 1823 on somewhat similar plans. In England Lord Brougham and the set of people around him were discussing the "march of intellect," and had established a Society for the Promotion of Useful Knowledge, whose name has lived after it. I may say here, in a parenthesis, that the first time I ever heard of the "march of intellect" was when I saw a very funny play, in which a clever boy named Burke was the hero in the "march of intellect." He appeared in half a dozen characters, to teach half a dozen subjects ; and it was a capital satire on the idea that everything could be taught by professors. Mr. Webster, Mr. Edward Everett, my father, and other gentlemen in their position established a society in Boston which did the same thing. The reign of Lyceums and Mechanics' Institutes had begun. Briefly, there was the real impression that the kingdom of heaven was to be brought in by teaching people what were the relations of acids to alkalies, and what was the derivation of the word "cordwainer." If we only knew enough, it was thought, we should be wise enough to keep out of the fire, and we should not be burned.

So it was that any novelty, when it was presented at a school-room door, was even more apt to be accepted than it is now ; and, as every reader of these lines knows, such things are accepted pretty willingly now. So I remember that I was taught "geometry" when I was six years old—or that I thought I was—from a little book called "The Elements of Geometry." I could rattle off about isosceles triangles when I was six, as well as I can now. And I had other queer smattering bits of knowledge, useful or useless, which were picked up in the same way.

At school there was a school library, from which we borrowed books, because we liked the mechanism of it. We had much better books at home ; but of course it was good fun to have your name entered on a book, and to return them once a week, and so on.

My father was one of the best teachers I ever knew. When he had a moment, therefore, from other affairs to give to our education, it was always well used ; and we doubtless owed a great deal to him which we afterwards did not know how to account for. Among other such benefactions, I owe it that for these three or four years, when really I had nothing to do but to grow physically, I was placed with a simple, foolish man for a teacher, and not with one of the drivers, who had plans and would want to make much of us. Among other notions of my father, right or wrong as the case may be, was this : that a boy could pick up the rudiments of language quite early in life. So the

master was told that Edward Webster and I,
and perhaps some other boys, were to be
taught the paradigms of the Latin grammar at
once. We also had given to us little Latin
books, which we spelled away upon. One was
a translation of Campe's German version of
"Robinson Crusoe" into Latin. It was
thought that the interest of the book would
induce us to learn the meaning of the words.
But the truth was, we were familiar with
Defoe's "Robinson Crusoe," and regarded this
as a low and foolish imitation, of which we made
a great deal of fun. All the same, the agony
with which some boys remember their first
studies of "*amo, amas, amat*," is wholly
unknown to me. I drifted into those things
simply, and by the time I was sent to the
Latin School the point had been gained, and
I knew my "*penna, pennæ, pennæ*," and my
"*amo, amas, amat*," as well as if I had been
born to them.

The Latin School stood, at that time, where
the lower part of Parker's Hotel is now, in
School Street. School Street received its name
from this school. At the beginning the school

was on the other side of the street, where the Franklin statue now stands. But when the King's Chapel people had increased so much, that they wanted to enlarge their little wooden tabernacle and carry their church farther down the street, about the middle of the last century, they applied to the town for the use of the school-house lot.

This was the occasion of a fierce battle in more than one town meeting. Really, the question divided the old line Puritans, or the people who held to their traditions, from the new people, who were either conscientious members of the Episcopal Church or were quite indifferent to the matter. But the town gave its consent, by a very small majority, to the removal of the school-house, and the King's Chapel people had to build a new school-house on the southern side of the street. This stood till 1814, when a larger house was built in the same place. This school-house made the side of what is now known as Chapman Place; but in my time this was called Cooke's Court, in honor of a certain Elisha Cooke, who was a very eminent man in colonial times. There were one or two old wooden houses in the court, one of which was covered with Virginia creeper, the first I ever saw. I remember thinking that the berries of the Virginia creeper were, in some sort, discovered by me, and that no one had known of their existence before, and I was disappointed that they proved to be such poor eating.

Above the school, on School Street, was a wooden house, with a garden in front of it, and further up still a new brick house, where, in the early part of these reminiscences, my father's family lived. From the back windows of this house, when I was a very little boy, I used to look out and see the boys at play. It will amuse the boys of the present generation to know that in summer most of them wore long calico gowns, quite like the gowns which ministers sometimes wear now, only without the flowing sleeves.

Boys were then admitted into the Latin School when they were nine years old. They were examined so far as to see if they could spell decently and whether they had some slight knowledge of arithmetic. As for writing, we were expected to learn that after we entered the school. Once there we were all put into the same class, and were set to studying our Latin grammar.

We always came to school early, all of the fun of the school being enjoyed before the bell rang. Different classes grouped in different corners of the neighborhood, and talked of the school news or the news of the day with the other fellows. We had some South End boys, who came to school highly excited one day with the announcement that an "omnibus" had been put upon Washington Street. No one had ever seen an omnibus before. This omnibus was called the Governor Brooks, and it had four horses, and it was twice as long as any omnibus which any Boston boy has seen in our streets now for twenty years. I felt, afterwards, quite sure that I rode up the long hill at Granada in Spain in the same omnibus, and I was terribly afraid that the linchpin might give way, but this may have been a delusion of mine. The first "omnibus" in the world was put on its work in Paris. It was

called "La Dame Blanche," from the White
Lady of Scott's novel of "The Monastery,"
about the year 1821.

We had not much room for playing, but we
might take a turn at tag or some other outdoor game before the school-bell rang. But at
last, at eight o'clock in summer and at nine
in winter, the bell began to ring. It rang for
five minutes, and before the end of the five
minutes every boy must be in his place. The
masters, four or five of them, had been standing in the meanwhile on the sidewalk in front
of the school door ; as the bell rang they bowed
to each other and repaired one by one to their
rooms.

About this bell there were various traditions, and its experience had, indeed, been
somewhat singular. I believe it had been the
bell of the Huguenot Church lower down on
the same street. It hung, as church bells
do, on the wheel in the cupola, but it had
long since been found that no rope on the
wheel would give to the bell the regular stroke
which for some reason was thought desirable.
Some strong, quick boy was therefore sent up

into the belfry, and he took hold of the tongue and struck it rapidly and sharply on the side of the bell. It may readily be seen that to do this for five minutes was quite an exhausting bit of physical labor, but, for all that, it was rather a privilege to be permitted to ring the bell. For, in compensation for doing so the boy was awarded certain credits on his conduct or recitation lists; and the boy who found himself going to the bad, in his studies or by any other bad marks, would ask to be assigned to the bell that he might work off these misdemeanors by the diligence of his bell-ringing. Some boys rang the bell well, some rang it badly, and a certain distinction attached to the business. I remember perfectly that, when on some occasion the bell-boy was absent, Mr. Dillaway, looking around for a substitute, sent me up into the belfry; but I made wretched work of the bell, and was not sorry to be relieved before a minute was over by some more stalwart boy who was more used to the business.

By the time the bell struck its last stroke every boy would be in his seat. The boys of the present generation have little idea what such seats were. At first they were simply long benches with what we call long "forms" in front. About midway of my school career, there were substituted for these benches separate desks, somewhat like what boys have now, but with the very hardest and smallest seat which was ever contrived for an unfortunate boy to wriggle upon. Still we could open the desks and support them with our heads while we pretended to be arranging our books. No school-boy who has ever had the felicity of such a desk, needs to be told what various orgies we could carry on under such shelter of protection.

A certain good-natured courtesy assigned to our school as a teacher of penmanship one of the old masters who was supposed to have outlived his usefulness in the "grammar school." This was Mr. Jonathan Snelling. We used to call him familiarly "Old Johnny Snelling," but we always treated him with the respect which was due to an old man. The days of quill pens had not gone by, and it was then a part of a boy's or girl's education to know

how to make a pen well—an accomplishment
which, I am afraid, is not now possessed by all
the readers of these lines. Johnny Snelling had
his own little room apart from the room of the
head-master, and the boys in that room went
in·to him to write ; but the other boys wrote
in different hours assigned for the purpose,
and Johnny Snelling went from room to room
to give them their instruction. For me, I
wrote wretchedly, and was always marked very
low on the calendar, but I would persuade this
good old gentleman to assign to me copies
in German text or old English or the other
variations from the deadly monotony of the
copybook, rather in the hope that I might
conciliate the masters, by the enterprise of
this break out into new fields. At all events
this was some variety, and as I have said it was
on the monotony of school life that my dislike
of it was founded.

I entered the school in 1831, being then nine
years old. That was the minimum for the
entrance of boys at that time, and the course
was five years. I saw Mr. Leverett, who was
the principal when I was admitted, but in the

course of a few weeks he left the school to the
charge of Mr. Charles Knapp Dillaway, who is
well remembered by everyone who has had
anything to do with education in Boston for
the last sixty years. I may say in passing that
I was permitted to speak at his funeral, and I
could not but remember then that, from the
time when he entered the Latin School in 1818
till he died in 1889, he had been personally
connected more or less distinctly with our
system of public education. He had, therefore, seen the working of that system for more
than a quarter part of the period since it was
established by Winthrop and his companions
in 1635.

The system of the school was rigid, but I do
not think boys object to rigidity. It carried
to the extreme the cultivation of verbal memory. We had a very bad Latin grammar,
which I suppose was the best there was, made
by Mr. Gould himself from Principal Adam's
"Latin Grammar," which was used in all
English schools. "Principal Adam" is the
Edinburgh Adam of whom you read in Walter
Scott and other Scotch books. The late

Joseph Gardner, laughing about such things a few years ago, said to me, "I can remember the block on which I was standing in the Place Vendôme in Paris, when, as by a revelation, it occurred to me that Andrews and Stoddard's "Latin Grammar" was made from the Latin language, and that the Latin language was not made from Andrews and Stoddard's grammar, as up to that moment I had always supposed."

I am quite clear that I went well through the Latin School with the distinct feeling that Adam's grammar stated the eternal truth with regard to the language, and that Cicero and the rest of them had had to adapt themselves to it. I cannot think that the masters thought so, but I doubt if they cared much about it, and certainly they left that impression on the minds of the pupils. The first year of the little boys was spent in committing the words of this grammar to memory. Unless a boy were singularly advanced he had no school-book in hand from September to the next August excepting this Latin grammar. I cannot conceive of any system more disposed to

make him hate the language; and in fact
about half the boys withdrew from the school,
as not having "a gift for language," before
they had been there two years. These were
generally the boys of quick and bright minds,
who went off "into business," as it was called,
because they were thought not fit to be
scholars. The professional lines of life thus
lost those who would have been ornaments in
whatever profession they had chosen, simply
because those lads had not the verbal memory
to remember and recall long lists of words,
which Adam had noticed, such, for one instance
in a thousand, as had or had not an *i* before
um in the genitive plural.

I will say in passing, what I have often
had occasion to say in public, that it would be
easy to prepare a bright boy or girl of sixteen
years of age to pass the Harvard Greek
entrance examination in four months of interested study.

But I do not propose to go into the niceties
of education in these papers. Thanks to the
prescience of my father, of which I have
spoken, I was put in with the ten-year-old

boys, who had ground through this mill. Till this moment I am their inferior in certain of those details of words to which I have referred, but I enjoyed life at school a great deal better than they did.

The "march of intellect" fad had not swept over Boston without bringing in the German notions about gymnasiums. Dr. Lieber arrived, an exile from Germany, with Dr. Beck, who was also an exile, and they established a swimming school where Brimmer Street is now, and a gymnasium in Tremont Street—then called Common Street—at the corner of West Street. That place was then called the "Washington Gardens." Mr. Hartwell, in his recent interesting essay on gymnastics in Boston, says that the first year Lieber's gymnasium in the Washington Gardens had two hundred pupils, which increased to four hundred in the second, and in the third year he had four pupils. These figures show only too fatally what was the fall of the athletic thermometer. More learned people than I must say, whether the system of gymnastics carried on by fixed machinery ever maintains its popularity for a long time, unless it is seconded by athletics such as we now class under that name, and by a certain rivalry.

My brother Nathan, to whom I owe most of what I am and have been in the world, was entered as one of the pupils in the Washington Gardens gymnasium. It must have been in the year 1827, or possibly 1828, that he took me with him there. All that I remember about it is my terror when I had climbed up a ladder and cut off my retreat. I had seen the other boys climb between the rounds and slide down the pole which supported the ladder, and I wished to do this. I got through the rounds and then was afraid to slide. But a competent teacher came up, instructed me in the business, and I won the high courage by which to loosen my feet from the rounds and slide safely down. I went home to tell this story with delight, but never repeated the experiment.

At the same time—and I think this shows the courage with which our education was carried on—I made my first essays in riding on horseback. My father owned a handsome horse, with which he took our mother and some one of the children out to ride on half-holidays. On some occasions another horse, which was called the "Work-bench" from his quiet habits—white, I recollect—was taken with us, saddled. This was that "we boys" might learn to ride. We were not permitted to ride in the streets in town, and father would ride the horse out so far, while my mother drove the chaise. But once in the country the boy mounted, and followed the chaise for the afternoon tour. At five years old I was so small that my feet would not reach the stirrups, and I rode with my feet in the straps which sustained the stirrups. All went well till, in South Boston, as we came home, some boys stoned my horse, and he ran and I was thrown. I remember repeating the experiment with the same success and failure, and it ended in my poor father having to ride the "Work-bench" home, while I ignominiously returned in the chaise as I had started.

The drift for athletics had swept over the Latin School also, and the square yard behind

the school, which seemed immense, but must
have been only thirty feet in each measure-
ment, was fitted up with a vaulting-horse, parallel bars, and so on.   But, as the fad wore
itself out, the boys were permitted to destroy
these things ; and when I entered the school,
in 1831, there were only the vaulting-horse
and, perhaps, a pair of parallel bars left ; and
these gradually disappeared from the curriculum.   This play-ground was the only play-
ground of the school, and was accessible only
to the boys in the lowest room.   Upstairs we
were confined to a very limited passage-way, I
might call it, at recess, in which we used to
play "tug-of-war," though we never called it
by that name.   Practically the recesses were
very short, for the simple reason that they did
not like to have us in the street.

Earlier than this, I can remember, when I
was only four or five years old, that we looked
from the windows of the house out upon the
street, to see the sports of the boys there,
when rather more liberty was granted them.
Among these sports I remember distinctly
seeing the older boys kick their pails to

pieces at the end of the school term. They would subscribe for pails in which to keep the water which they wanted to drink in the hot days; and when the term was done, not wishing to leave the pails to their successors, they kicked them about the sidewalk and street until they were ruined.

To this school we repaired at eight o'clock in the morning for the months between April and October, and at nine o'clock from the 1st of October to the 1st of April. School lasted till twelve o'clock, excepting for the little boys, who, in the latter part of my time, were "let out" at eleven o'clock. School began again at three, and lasted, in winter, as long as there was light, and in summer till six o'clock. I remember the bitter terror which we had one afternoon, which must have been in May, 1833, when we were to go and see Fanny Kemble in the evening. As it happened, the school committee chose to come that afternoon for an examination, and our class was kept in for the completion of the examination after six o'clock. We sat there terrified for fear the examination would last until the play began in the Tremont Theatre, hard by. I am afraid the boys of to-day would consider it rather hard lines, if they were ever kept at school till the beginning of their theatrical entertainment.

In Mr. Freeman Clarke's autobiography there is a charming passage about his stay at this school. He does not in the least overstate the admirable democratic effect of the whole thing. We were side by side with the sons of the richest and most prominent men in Boston; we were side by side with the sons of day laborers, I suppose. The odd thing about it is that we did not know, and we did not care, whose sons they were. They were all dressed alike, they spoke equally good English, their hands were equally clean, and all we knew of them was that one fellow was at the head of the class, and one was not. There was a charming boy named Carleton—Charles Muzzey Carleton—who was at the head of my class. He was a pure, manly, upright, gentlemanly fellow, a much better boy than any of the rest of us were, and we therefore chose to nickname him "Piety Carleton." I am afraid we made him very unhappy by the nickname, but he bore himself in just as manly a way in spite of it. I wish I had known him as a man —and I ought here to record my shame that we treated him so ill.

It was a queer transition time for schools. The present murderous and absurd system of "examinations" was wholly unknown. Each master got along as well as he could with his boys, and the boys got along as well as they could with the master. There was one head-master, a sub-master, and two others, who were called ushers on the printed catalogue, but were never so called by the boys. Whatever the age of these gentlemen, they were always called "old." It was "Old Dillaway," "Old Gardner," "Old Streeter," or "Old Benjamin." I now know that the oldest of them was not thirty-five, and that most of them were not twenty-five.

We were changed from room to room, seldom staying in one room more than three months, but the highest class was always with the head-master. I remember one occasion— I was about ten years old—when, to our

delight, we were ordered upstairs from the
"English room." We were pleased because
it was known that the new master there was
very easy, and that the "fellows did as they
chose." It was so, indeed. I recollect my
amazement when I saw Hancock cross the
room without leave, make a snowball from
the snow in a pail, and carry it back ostenta-
tiously to place it on the front of his desk.
The snow was provided for use on the stove,
where there was a provision for a pan of
water. From this he then made little snow-
balls with which to pelt the other boys, all
without interruption from the master.

But other things went on with the same freedom, which were of more import. I was seated
next to Hayward, whom I then met for the first
time, and who has since been a life-long friend.
His class was reading Cicero's orations. He
asked me what I knew about Cicero ; and,
when I told him I knew nothing, he kindly
went into a somewhat elaborate history of his
life and analysis of his character as they
appeared to a boy of his age. He has forgotten
this, but I remember it perfectly. It seems to

me that this extempore private lecture must
have lasted the whole afternoon. The poor
master made no sort of interference with it,
probably glad if two of his scholars were doing
nothing worse than talking.

But alas, and alas! this paradise of King
Log came to an end in a day or two. This
amiable gentleman, whose name I have forgotten, was removed, and Francis Gardner
was put in his place. For forty years after
he was master in that school, and is now well
known as a distinguished classical teacher and
editor. That was his baptism in a school-
master's life, and a baptism of fire it was.
We were afterwards intimate friends, and he
told me once that his first month, when he was
bringing those wild-cat boys into order, was
the hardest experience of his life.

In the English room, according to the absurd
theory of many schools, the whole class was
kept together, without any reference to what
they knew of the subject. That is to say, we
were classed for our knowledge of Latin, and
nobody seemed to care how much or how little
we knew of arithmetic. I used to do " the

sums" and write down the numerical answers
in advance, so far as my slate would hold
them.   I was fond of arithmetic, and so I would
be days ahead of the class.   Such was also the
case with Richard Storrs Willis, the eminent
musician, who sat by me.   He brought to
school Kettell's "Specimens of American
Poetry," a book of that time, in three closely
printed octavo volumes.   We read the three
volumes through, and a deal of trash there is
in them.   Still it was better than doing nothing ; and so I suppose the master thought, for
he never interfered.

To me this was all a curious double life.   I
was on perfect terms of companionship with
the fellows in school in recess and in the few
minutes before school.   But as soon as school
was over I rushed home, without these companions, to join my brother Nathan, who has
been spoken of, for the occupations vastly
more important, which I will describe in
another chapter.   The other fellows would
urge us to go down on the wharves, as they
did.   The fathers of most of them were in mercantile life, for Boston was still largely a ship-

ping town. I can remember asking one of them what we should do on the wharves, with a horrified feeling which I have to this day about any vague future entertainment of which the lines are not indicated. He said, "Oh, we can go about the vessels, we can talk with the men." Perhaps they would be landing molasses, and we could dip straws in the bung-holes ; or once a cask had broken open, and the fellows had gathered up brown sugar in their hands. To this day, when I hear of persons going abroad or anywhere else in search of an undefined amusement, I imagine them dipping straws into casks of West India molasses, and then drawing those straws through their mouths.

For me and my brother such temptations were idle. Till the last year of my school life we had more attractive work at home. In that year Edward Renouf, afterwards an Episcopal clergyman, told us that he had access to the wood wharves on Front Street, near where the United States Hotel now stands. He said there were no other fellows there. For some reason not known to me there were no wharfingers or

other attendants.   With him, and possibly
with Atkins, we used to spend hours on those
wharves.   The Boston reader will please
observe that Beach Street means a street on
the beach, and that Harrison Avenue, then
called Front Street, was the front of that part
of the town.   Why there were no keepers on
those wharves I never asked, and do not know.
Whether what we did were right or wrong in
the view of magistrates I do not know.   I do
know that it was morally and eternally right,
because we thought it was.   That is one of the
queer things about a boy's conscience.   I do
not remember that, till the time when I dictate
these words, for nearly sixty years, it has once
occurred to me to ask whose was the property
we used on these occasions, or what the owners
would have said to our use of it.   But they
did not suffer much, if at all.   There were
great stacks of hemlock bark, which was then
coming into use in winter as kindling for
anthracite coal.   You could take one of these
pieces of bark, three or four feet long, bore
three holes for masts, and fit this hull with
three masts made from shingles or laths.   Stiff

wrapping-paper made good sails, and writing-books were big enough for topsails. Then you could sail them from wharf to wharf, on voyages much more satisfactory than the shorter voyages of the Frog Pond. I do not know but that, with a favorable western wind, one might come out at Sallee, on the coast of Morocco, with the location of which we were familiar from the experience of *Robinson Crusoe* and *Xury*. We knew much more of that port than of Lisbon, Oporto, or Bordeaux.

But this is an excursus which belongs rather to the chapter on amusements. The home rule was absolute, and always obeyed, that we must report at home as soon as school was done. This rule undoubtedly interfered with excursions to the wharves, which, indeed, had my father been a shipping merchant, might have been more frequent. School life of itself had little to relieve it of its awful monotony. Saturday was better than the other days, because we all went upstairs into the master's room to hear the declamations. Every boy spoke from the stage once a month. And here I have heard William Evarts, Fletcher Webster,

Mayor Prince, Thomas Dawes—ah! and many others who have been distinguished since as orators.   Phillips, Hillard, Sumner, and the Emersons were a little before my time, but I have seen the prize exercises of all of them among the treasures of the school.

I remember perfectly the first time I spoke. It must have been in September, 1831.   At my mother's instigation I spoke a little poem by Tom Moore, long since forgotten by everybody else, which I had learned and spoken at the other school.   It is a sort of ode, in which Moore abuses some poor Neapolitan wretches because they had made nothing of a rebellion against the Austrians.   I stepped on the stage, frightened, but willing to do as I had been told, made my bow, and began:

Ay, down to the dust with them, slaves as they are!

I had been told that I must stamp my foot at the words, "Down to the dust with them," and I did, though I hated to, and was sore afraid.   Naturally enough all the other boys, one hundred and fifty of them, laughed at such an exhibition of passion from one of the smallest of their number. All the same, I plodded on; but alas! I came inevitably to the other line:

If there linger one spark of their fire, tread it out!

and here I had to stamp again, as much to the boys' amusement as before. I did not get a "good mark" for speaking then, and I never did afterwards. But the exercise did what it was meant to do, that is, it taught us not to be afraid of the audience. And this, so far as I know, is all of elocution that can be taught, or need be tried for. In college, it was often very droll when the time came for one of the Southern braggarts to speak at an exhibition. For we saw then the same young man who had always blown his own trumpet loudly, and been cock of the walk in his own estimation— we saw him with his knees shaking under him on the college platform because he had to speak in the presence of two hundred people. I owe to the public school, and to this now despised exercise of declamation, that ease before an audience which I share with most New

Englanders.   This is to say that I owe to it the great pleasure of public speaking when there is anything to say.   I think most public men will agree with me that this is one of the most exquisite pleasures of life.

CHAPTER III.

JOY, joy, joy! Of a hot summer day in June, when I was nine years old, I was asked how I would like to learn to swim. Little doubt in the mind of any boy who reads this what my answer was. I and my elder brother, who was twelve, were to be permitted to go to the swimming school. This was joy enough to have that year marked with red in our history.

As I have said, Dr. Francis Lieber, who had been exiled from Germany a few years before, had come to Boston, and had established first his gymnasium and then his swimming school. Swimming schools were and are thoroughly established on the continent of Europe, and the Germans have a special reputation for skill in swimming. With the gymnasium I had little or nothing to do but what

I have told.   I was, indeed, quite too small to
be put through its exercises.

The swimming school was in water which
flowed where Brimmer Street and the houses
behind it are now built.   It was just such a
building as the floating baths are now which
the city maintains, but that it enclosed a much
larger space.   Of this space a part had a floor
so that the water flowed through ; the depth
was about five feet.   To little boys like me it
made little difference that there was this floor,
for we could be as easily drowned in five feet
of water as if there were fifteen.

With great delight I carried down my little
bathing drawers, which were marked with my
own number so that they might always hang
upon my peg.   With the drawers and my
towels I proceeded to a little cell, just such as
bathers have at South Boston now, with the
great advantage, however, that its door was
made of sail-cloth.   You selected a cell on the
northern side, so that when you went into the
water you could draw your sail-cloth into the
sun, and the sun would heat it well through ;
then, after your bath, you stood wrapped up

in this warm linen shroud, and the luxury was considered exquisite.

So soon as you were undressed and ready— and this meant in about one minute—you took your turn to be taught. A belt was put around you under your arms; to this belt a rope was attached, and you were told to jump in. You jumped in and went down as far as gravity chose to take you, and were then pulled up by the rope. The rope was then attached to the end of a long belt, and you were swung out upon the surface of the water. Then began the instruction.

"O-n-e ;—two, three : " the last two words spoken with great rapidity—"one" spoken very slowly. This meant that the knees and feet were to be drawn up very slowly, but were to be dashed out very quickly, and then the heels brought together as quickly.

Boys who were well built for it and who were quick learned to swim in two or three lessons. Slender boys and little boys who had not much muscular force—and such was I—were a whole summer before they could be trusted without the rope. But the training was excellent, and from the end of that year till now I have been entirely at home in the water. I think now that scientific and systematic training in swimming is a very important part of public instruction, and I wish we could see it introduced everywhere where there is responsible oversight of boys at school.

CHAPTER IV.

LIFE AT HOME.

I AM certainly not writing my autobiography ; but I cannot give any idea of how boys lived in the decade when I was a boy—that is, in the years between 1826 and 1836—without giving a chapter to home life as I saw it. In passing I will say that I first remember the figures 1826, thus combined, as I saw them on the cover of Thomas's Almanac of 1827. Here Time, with the figures 1827 on his head, was represented as mowing in a churchyard, where a new stone with the figures 1826 was prominent ; 1825, 1824, and the others were on stones somewhat overgrown by grass and sunken in the ground. The conceit seemed to me admirable, and the date fixed itself on my memory.

I was born in a house which stood where Parker's larger lunch-room now fronts the

Tremont House.   We moved from this house
to that on the corner of School Street, lately
purchased by Mr. Parker to enlarge his hotel,
and in 1828 we moved again to the new house,
which was, and is, No. 1 Tremont Place.   It
is now two or three stories higher than it was
then ; but some parts of the interior are not
changed.   Behind it was a little yard, with a
wood-house, called a "shed," on top of which
the clothes were dried.   This arrangement
was important for our New England childhood.

I was the youngest of four children who
made the older half of a large family.   By a
gap between me and my brother Alexander,—
who afterwards was lost in the government
service in Pensacola,—"we four" were separated from the "three little ones."   It is
necessary to explain this in advance, in a history which is rather a history of young life in
Boston than of mine alone.

My father, as I have said, was an experi-
enced teacher in young life, and he never lost
his interest in the business of education.   My
mother had a genius for education, and it is a
pity that, at an epoch in her life when she

wanted to open a girls' school, she was not permitted to do so. They had read enough of the standard books on education to know how much sense there was in them, and how much nonsense. Such books were about in the house, more or less commented on by us young critics as we grew big enough to dip into them.

At the moment I had no idea that any science or skill was expended on our training. I supposed I was left to the great American proverb which I have already cited : "Go as you please." But I have seen since that the hands were strong which directed this gay team of youngsters, though there was no stimulus we knew of, and though the touch was velvet. An illustration of this was in that wisdom of my father in sending me for four years to school to a simpleton.

The genius of the whole, shown by both my father and mother, came out in the skill which made home the happiest place of all, so that we simply hated any engagement which took us elsewhere, unless we were in the open air. I have said that I disliked school, and that I did not want to go down on the wharves, even with that doubtful bribe of the molasses casks. At home we had an infinite variety of amusements. At home we might have all the other boys, if we wished. At home, in our two stories, we were supreme. The scorn of toys which is reflected in the Edgeworth books had, to a certain extent, its effect on the household. But we had almost everything we wanted for purposes of manufacture or invention. Whalebone, spiral springs, pulleys, and catgut, for perpetual motion or locomotive carriages ; rollers and planks for floats—what they were I will explain—all were obtainable. In the yard we had parallel bars and a high crosspole for climbing. When we became chemists we might have sulphuric acid, nitric acid, litmus paper, or whatever we desired, so our allowance would stand it. I was not more than seven years old when I burned off my eyebrows by igniting gunpowder with my burning-glass. I thought it was wisest not to tell my mother, because it might shock her nerves, and I was a man, thirty years old, before she heard of it. Such playthings as these, with very careful restrictions on the

"I WAS NOT MORE THAN SEVEN YEARS OLD WHEN I BURNED OFF MY EYEBROWS."—*Page* 62.

amount of powder, with good blocks for building, quite an assortment of carpenter's tools, a work-bench good enough, printing materials *ad libitum* from my father's printing-office, furnished endless occupation.

Before I attempt any account of the home life which grew out of such conditions I must make a little excursus to describe the domestic service of those days, quite different from ours. I wish particularly to describe Fullum, who outlived the class to which he belonged, and had, when he died, in 1886, long been its last representative.

The few New England children who still read the Rollo books will have pleasant remembrances of *Jonas* and *Beechnut*, in whom Mr. Jacob Abbott has presented for posterity the hired boy of New England country life. In life in a little town like Boston this hired boy might grow to be the hired man, and, as in Fullum's exceptional case, might grow to be a hundred years old, or nearly that, without changing that condition. If that happened his presence in a family became a factor of importance to the growing children. In the case of Fullum, if, as he supposed, he was born in 1790, he was thirty-two years old when, in 1822, he took me in his arms when I was an hour old.

Fullum, then, had been a country lad, who came down from Worcester County to make his fortune. I do not know when, but it was before the time of the short war with England. He expected to be, and was, the hired boy and hired man in one and another Boston family. Early in the business he was in Mr. William Sullivan's service. He was driving Mr. Sullivan out of town, one day, when they found Roxbury Street blocked up by the roof of the old meeting-house, which had been blown into the street by the gale of September, 1815. Afterward he was in Daniel Webster's service, and here also he took care of horses and carriages. He was a born tyrant, and it was always intimated that Mr. Webster did not fancy his rule. Anyway he came from the Websters to us, I suppose when Mr. Webster went to Congress, in the autumn of 1820. And, in one fashion or another, he lived with our family, as a most faithful vassal or tyrant, for

sixty-six years from that time.   I say "vassal
or tyrant," for this was a pure piece of feudal-
ism; and in the feudal system the vassal is
often a tyrant, while the master is almost
always a slave.   So is it that the memories of
my boyhood are all mixed up with memories
of Fullum.

I have spoken of him in connection with
Miss Whitney's school.   Here was a faithful
man Friday, who would have died for any of
us, so strong was his love for us, yet who
insisted on rendering his service very much
in his own way.   If my father designed a
wooden horse for me, to be run on four
wheels, after the fashion of what were called
velocipedes in those days, he would make the
drawings, but it would be Fullum's business
to take them to the carpenter's and see the
horse made.   If we were to have heavy hoops
from water-casks, Fullum was the person who
conducted the negotiation for them.   There
was no harm in the tutorship to which we
were thus intrusted.   He never used a pro-
fane or impure word while he was with us
children; and as he was to us an authority in

all matters of gardening, of carpentry, of driving and the care of horses, we came to regard
him as, in certain lines, omniscient and omnipotent. If now the reader will bear in mind
that this omniscient and omnipotent person,
at once the Hercules and the Apollo of our
boyhood, could not read, write, or spell so
well as any child four years old who had been
twelve months at Miss Whitney's school, that
reader may understand why a certain scorn of
book-learning sometimes stains these pages,
otherwise so pure. And if the same reader
should know that this same Fullum always
spoke in superlatives, and multiplied every
figure with which he had to do by hundreds
or by thousands, he may have a key to a certain habit of exaggeration which has been
detected in the present writer. "They was
ten thousand men tryin' to git in. But old
Reed, he wouldn't let um." This would be
his way of describing the effort of four or five
men to enter some place from which Reed,
the one constable of Boston, meant to keep
them out.

The reader must excuse this excursus, for I

think it necessary. I think it necessary for
the civilized child to be kept in touch, in his
childhood, with animals and with savages.
Fullum was the person through whom savage
life touched ours. To Fullum, largely, we
owed it that we were neither prigs nor dudes.
We had no cats, nor dogs, nor birds ; and
Fullum's place in these reminiscences is far
more important than is that of any pet, any
school-master, or any minister.

The oldest child of "us four" was but
four years and nine months older than the
youngest. She had, as I have said, received,
and deserved, at Miss Whitney's a medal
given to the "most amiable." Next to her
came a boy, then another girl, and then this
writer. The movements of "us four" had
much in common ; but at school and in most
plays the boys made one unit and the girls
another, to report every evening to one
another. It is to the boyhood experiences
that these pages belong.

But it was a Persian and Median rule of
that household, which I recommend to all
other households, that after tea there were to

be no noisy games. The children must sit
down at the table—there was but one—and
occupy themselves there till bedtime. It has
been well said that the ferocity of infancy is
such that, were its strength equal to its will,
it would long ago have exterminated the
human race. This is true. And it is to be
remarked, also, that the strength of infancy,
and of boyhood and girlhood, is very great.
Thus is it that, unless some strict rules are
laid down for limiting its use and the places
of its exhibition, and kept after they are laid
down, the death of parents, and of all persons
who have passed the age of childhood, may
be expected at any moment. One of such
rules was this of which I have spoken.

Everybody of whom we knew anything
dined at one or two o'clock in Boston then.
After dinner men went back to their places of
business. At six, or possibly as late as seven
in summer, came "tea." After tea, as I have
said, the children of this household gathered
round the table. Fullum came in and took
away the tea things, folded the cloth and put
it away. Our mother then drew up her chair

to the drawer of the table, probably with a
baby in her arms awaiting the return of its
nurse. We four drew up our chairs on the
other sides. Then we might do as we chose—
teetotum games, cards of all sorts, books,
drawing, or evening lessons, if there were any
such awful penalty resulting from the sin of
Adam and Eve. But nobody might disturb
anyone else.

Drawing was the most popular of the occupations, and took the most of our time and
thought. The provisions for it were very
simple, and there was only the faintest pretence at instruction. There was one particular brand of lead pencils, sold by one particular
grocer in West Street at twelve cents a dozen.
These were bought at this wholesale rate, and
kept in the drawer. One piece of India rubber
was also kept there for the crowd. As we
gathered at the table, a quarter-sheet of foolscap was given to each child and to each
guest—as regularly as a bit of butter had been
given half an hour before—and one pencil.

The reader must imagine the steady flow
of voices. "Who's got the India rubber?"

"Here it is under the Transcript." "This horse looks as if he were walking on foot-balls." "Oh, you mustn't draw his shoes ; you never see his shoes !" "I wish I knew how to draw a chaise." "I don't see how they make pictures of battles. My smoke covers up all the soldiers." Battle pieces, indeed, were, as usual with children, the favorite compositions. We were not so far from the last war with England as the children of to-day are from the Civil War.

Perhaps two of us put together our paper, folded it and pinned it in the fold, and then made a magazine. Of magazines there were two—*The New England Herald*, composed and edited by the two elders of the group, and *The Public Informer*, by my sister Lucretia and me. I am afraid that the name "Public Informer" was suggested wickedly to us little ones, when we did not know that those words carry a disagreeable meaning. But when we learned this, afterwards, we did not care. I think some of the Everetts, my uncles, had had a boy newspaper with the same name. When things ran with perfect regularity *The*

New England Herald was read at the break-
fast-table one Monday morning, and *The Public
Informer* the next Monday morning. But
this was just as it might happen. They were
published when the editors pleased, as all
journals should be, and months might go by
without a number. And there was but one
copy of each issue. It would be better if this
could be said of some other journals.

Once a year prizes were offered at school
for translations or original compositions. We
always competed, not to say were made to
compete, by the unwritten law of the family.
This law was simply that we could certainly
do anything if we wanted to and tried. I
remember a long rhythmical version I made of
the story of the flood, in Ovid, and another of
Phaeton. Where Dryden makes Jupiter say,
"Short exhortations need," I remember that
my halting line jumbled along into the ten
syllables, "Long exhortations are not needed
here." I stinted myself in this translation
to four lines before dinner and four lines after
tea ; and by writing eight lines thus, in fifty
days I accomplished the enterprise. I would

come home from the swimming school ten
minutes earlier because this translation was to
be made ; and, while Fullum was setting the
table for dinner, I would stand at the sideboard.   There was always an inkstand on it,
with two or three quill pens.   I took out the
poem from the upper drawer of the sideboard,
which I never see to this moment without
thinking of Ovid.   Then I wrote my four lines,
such as they were, put the manuscript away
again, and proceeded to dinner.

Other boys and other girls liked to come in to
such an evening congress as I have described,
but nothing was changed in the least because
the visitor came, excepting that room was made
at the table.   He or she had a quarter-sheet of
foolscap, like the others.

This literature is connected with that of the
world by one reminiscence, which belongs as
late as some of the very last of these evening
sessions.   One evening my father came in from
his room, which was next to that we sat in, with
the London *Morning Chronicle*.   He pointed
out an article and said : " Read that to them,
Edward ; it will make them laugh."   And I

read the first account of *Sam Weller* as he
revealed himself to *Mr. Pickwick*. Of course
we all laughed, as thousands have done since.
But I said sadly : "What a shame that we
shall never hear of *Sam Weller* again!" This
must have been in the college vacation of the
spring of 1837.

I must not give the idea, however, by speaking of these evenings thus that our lives
were specially artistic or literary. They were
devoted to play, pure and simple, with no
object but having a good time. The principal
part of the attics—or, as we called them, gar-
rets—in every house we lived in was surren-
dered to us boys. In Tremont Place we had
the valuable addition of a dark cockloft over
the garret chambers. It had no windows, but
was all the better place to sit and tell stories
in. Then we controlled the stairs to the roof,
and we spent a good deal of time, in the summer days, on the ridge-pole. There were not
twenty houses in Boston on higher land, so
that from this point we commanded a good
view of the harbor. I was amused the other
day when an infantile correspondent of a New

York newspaper asked how Napoleon could have used a telegraph before what is called Mr. Morse's invention, for as early as 1831 we read all the telegraphic signals of all the vessels arriving in Boston harbor, and the occasional semaphoric signals on the lookout on Central Wharf.

About the year 1830, under the pressure of the "march of intellect," were published some books for young children from which the present generation is profiting largely. There were "The Boy's Own Book," "The Girl's Own Book," "The American Girl's Own Book," and "The Young Lady's Own Book," each of them excellent in its way. I think "The Boy's Own Book," which has since been published with the double title "An Encyclopædia for Boys," led the way in this affair; and I still regard it as rather the best of the series. It had subdivisions for indoor games, outdoor games, gymnastics, chemistry, chess, riddles, riding, walking, and I think driving, boxing, and fencing. Perhaps there were more heads, but these were those which occupied our attention most. Somebody made

me a New Year's present of this book in the
year 1830 or 1831, and from that moment it was
the text-book of the attic. Professor Andrews
and President Eliot would feel their hair growing gray, if for five minutes they were obliged
to read the chemistry which soaked into us
from this book. Whoever wrote it still used
the old nomenclature a good deal. We knew
nothing of HO, and little of the proportions in
which they go into the constitution of things.
We read of "oil of vitriol" and "muriatic
acid," and had other antiquarian names for
agents and reagents. All the same, the book
gave us experiments which we could try—
taught us how to manufacture fireworks in a
fashion, and even suggested to us the painting
of our own magic lantern slides. Our apparatus was of the most limited kind. It
was a high festival day when one went
down to Gibbens' grocer's shop and bought
for three cents an empty Florence flask;
this was the retort of that simple chemistry. In connection with this, like all other
boys of that time known to me, we made what
were called electrical machines, which gave us

good sparks and Leyden jar shocks quite sufficient to satisfy the guests who visited us.

It is in connection with one of these machines
that I remember one of my mother's gospels.
I was trying to catch a fly, to give him an electric shock, and she would not permit me.   I
pleaded in vain that it would not hurt him, but
she said : "It would certainly not give him
pleasure, and it might give him pain."

My father was a civil engineer, somewhat in
advance of his time.   He was the first person
to propose the railroad system of Massachusetts ; and that system would not be what it is,
but for his work for it, in season and out of
season.   I cannot remember the time when we
did not have a model railway in the house ; in
earlier years it was in the parlor, so that he
might explain to visitors what was meant by a
car running upon rails.   I can still see the
sad, incredulous look, which I understood then
as well as I should now, with which some intelligent person listened kindly, and only in manner
implied that it was a pity that so intelligent a man as he should go crazy.   His crazi-
ness, fortunately, led his associates, and in the

year 1831, after endless reverses, a charter was given for the incorporation of the Boston and Worcester Railway. In the earlier proposals for such work it was always suggested that horses should be the moving power. In point of fact the first railway, which carried the Quincy granite from Quincy to the sea, was operated by the weight of the descending trains, which pulled up the empty cars. I was with him, as a little boy, sitting on a box in the chaise, when he drove out once to see the newly laid Quincy track, and I perfectly remember his trying with his foot the steadiness of the rail where it crosses the road to Quincy. His tastes, of course, led ours. There was a lathe in the house, which we were permitted to run under severe conditions; and we very early made our own locomotives, which were propelled by whalebone springs.

But the carriage we liked most was the "float." I have never seen it in the plays of other boys, though perhaps it is well known. For a good float you want a board a foot wide, an inch thick, and four feet long. You want two rollers, which had better be of hard wood,

each a foot long and an inch or more in diameter ; two inches would be better than one, but
you take what you can get ; a broomstick
furnishes two or three good ones. Placing
these rollers two feet apart on the ground, you
put the float upon them, with one roller at the
end, and the other in the middle. You then
seat yourself carefully on the board, having
two paddles in your hands, made from shingles.
With these two paddles you will find that you
can propel yourself over any floor of reason-
able smoothness. You can even pass a thresh-
old, and you can run into the most unexpected
corners. If you have a companion on another
float in the same room, you can have naval
battles, or you can go to the assistance of ship-
wrecked crews. You can go forward or you
can go backward, every now and then running
a roller out, but skilfully placing it under the
float at such an angle as will direct you in the
way in which you wish to go afterwards. For
this game or sport you should not have too
many companions ; you should have a good
large attic or barn floor, and you should have
unlimited patience. You can make a float, of

course, out of a museum door, or out of any
plank that happens to be going. I remember
once, when we were hard pressed, one of my
companions went to sea in a soap box. But
what I have described is the ideal float for
young people.

We played all the tame games, such as
checkers, chess, loto, battledoor and shuttle-
cock, graces, vingt-et-un, cup and ball, coro-
nella, and the like, but I think under a certain protest. For that matter, I danced under
the same protest. I regarded all these as con-
cessions to the social order in which we lived,
and I obeyed that social order as I did in
going to school. But, precisely as I looked
upon school with a certain sense of con-
descension, I think we all looked upon these
games as being something provided for an
average public, while we supposed that all
children of sense invented their own games.

I have never, by the way, seen in print the
statement that our teetotum games of that
day were a survival of games of the same kind
running well back into the dark ages. In the
great German museum at Nuremberg I saw

such games of as early a date, I think, as the year 1300.   Any boy who will look at his tee-totum game of to-day, if such things still exist, will probably find that it comes out at 63.   This means that 63 is the "grand climac-teric," in the old theory of the climacterics ; and then, if he will look back, he will find that at 7, 14, 21, 28, and so on are the other climacterics.   All this belongs to those happy ages which knew nothing of modern science.

I have stated already the absolute rule that we must report at home before we went any-where to play after school.   I think this rule affected our lives a great deal more than my mother meant it should in laying it down. She simply wanted to know at certain stages of the day where her children were.   I do not recollect that she ever forbade our going any-where, where we wanted to.   But practically the rule worked thus : We rushed home from school, very likely with a plan on foot for the Common, or for some combined movement with the other boys.   We went into the house to re-port.   There was invariably gingerbread ready for us, which was made in immense quantities for the purpose. This luncheon was ready not only for us, but for any boys we might bring with us. When once we arrived at home the home attractions asserted themselves. There was some chemical experiment to be continued, or there was some locomotive to be displayed to another boy, or there had come in a new number of the *Juvenile Miscellany*. In a word, we were seduced up into the attic, and up in the attic we were very apt to stay. I once asked my mother what she supposed the mothers of the other boys said who came home with us and partook of luncheon and entered into our affairs. She simply said that that was their lookout, it was not hers. She was perfectly ready to provide luncheon for the crowd. I rather think that the other mothers knew that the boys were well off.

There were but few companions who were admitted into the profoundest mysteries of the attic. Edward Webster was one, who afterward died in command of a regiment in the Mexican War. My cousin John Durivage was one, and there were others whose companionship was not as long or as steady as that of these

two.   In the year 1829 my brother Nathan,
who was my adviser, teacher, companion, and
inspirer in everything, being three years older
than myself, went to the newly established
English High School for two years.   Here his
smattering of science and taste for mechanics
were fostered, and from such a laboratory as
was there he brought home suggestions for our
workshop.   I have always known that I am
thus largely indebted, at second hand, to the
suggestions which he received from Mr. Miles
and Mr. Sherwin there.   And this is not a bad
instance of the way in which the power of a
great educator extends itself beyond the lives
of the pupils whom he has under his eye at
school.

My father was editor of the *Daily Advertiser;* and in that day this meant that he
owned the whole printing plant, engaged all
the printers, and printed his own newspaper.
He was never a practical printer, but, with his
taste for mechanics, he understood all the processes of the business.   Not unnaturally this
grew into his establishing a book office, which
did as good work in its time as was done any-

where. The first American edition of Cicero's
" Republic," after the discovery of that book in
a Pompeian manuscript by Mai, was printed
by him. Naturally he went forward into the
study of power-press printing, and, at his suggestion, Daniel Treadwell made the first power
presses which worked to advantage in this
country. In the years between 1820 and 1825
the Boston Mill-dam was constructed, for the
purpose of making a water power out of the
tide power of the Back Bay. My father then
introduced power-press printing there, and
that printing-office was maintained until the
year 1836. When the time came he was president of the first type foundry in New England,
perhaps in America. All the arrangements
for these contrivances were, of course, interesting to his sons. So, as I have said, we had
type from the printing-office, and we all learned
to set type and to arrange it. When, in 1834,
my brother went to college, and I was left
alone, I used to repair every day to the book
office for my printing, and there learned the
case and all the processes of imposing scientifi-
cally. I used to work off my own books on a

hand press. I have never lost the memories of the case, and am rather fond of saying now that, if it were necessary, I could support my family as a compositor.

I would not have gone into this detail but that I am always urging people to let their boys have printing apparatus in early life, because I think it is such a good educator. The absolute accuracy that is necessary is good for a boy. The solid fact that 144 ems will go into a certain space, and will require that space, and that no prayers nor tears, hopes nor fears, will change that solid fact—this is most important. I do not mean the mere convenience to an author of being able to talk familiarly with the compositor who has his book in hand : that is a good thing. But I mean that human life in general has lessons to teach which every compositor requires which few other experiences of life teach so well. I think also that, as a study of English style, the school of Franklin and Horace Greeley is a good one.

For home reading we had the better magazines of that day, including the English *New Monthly*, which was then under the editorial

charge of Campbell.   We had the weekly literary newspapers which were beginning, such
as the *New World*, edited by Park Benjamin ;
the *Spirit of the Times*, which had a great deal
of sporting news ; the *Albion*, a weekly which
was made up of extracts from good foreign
papers.   I remember the issue of the last of
Scott's novels—" Anne of Geierstein," "Castle Dangerous," and " Count Robert of Paris."
There was a sort of grief in the family, as if a
near friend had died, or as if some one had
gone crazy, when " Castle Dangerous " and
"Count Robert" appeared, because they were
so poor.   The last part of " Harry and Lucy "
was published within our day, and we read of
those children almost as if they were personal
friends—a good deal as a younger generation
has read of *Rollo* and *Jonas*, and a certain
Susy in the Susy books.   Of course the physical science in " Harry and Lucy " had its
part in our philosophical experiments.   Miss
Edgeworth's " Helen " was published within
my memory, and we had friends who occasionally brought in letters from the Edgeworths
and read them.

We were all instinct with the love of nature and of the country, and of our excursions outside the old peninsula of Boston I will say something in another chapter. But we could hardly have lived without some sort of gardening at home—certainly not under my mother's lead. In the yard at the corner of School Street there was a very, very little space where we could plant seeds, and did. But when we came to Tremont Place there was no such space, and we were obliged to do as they did at Babylon. We each, therefore, had on the "shed," which was made for the drying of clothes, a raisin box filled with earth for our horticultural experiments. You can do a good deal with a raisin box, if you are careful and not too ambitious. Practically I planted morning-glories along one long side, with sweet peas between. These were to climb up on the posts. There is a tradition in the family that, when I was a boy of eight, I threw over a morning-glory to a baby six or eight months old, who was being carried by in the street, whom I married twenty-two years after. I need not say that this tradition, well founded as a matter of art, has no foundation in fact excepting that "it might have been." Behind the vines divide your box into even parts. The right-hand side is for agriculture: there you will plant your radishes and pepper-grass. The left-hand side is for flowers: here you can put in four rows ; for instance, touch-me-nots, flytrap, Venus' looking-glass, and ten-week stocks. I think we generally selected our seeds from something which seemed romantic in the name more than with any reference to what would be produced. I do not mean that one had the same things one summer which he had the year before.

These gardens, covering perhaps a square foot and a half each, were of the greatest interest to us. I remember we were very much amused when some children on the other side of the way, who lived in one of those elegant houses where the Bellevue now stands, whose terraces ran up the grades of the old Beacon Hill, said to us that they envied us our raisin boxes on the shed. From the same shed I observed the annular eclipse of the sun in the spring of 1829.

CHAPTER V.

WE were close by the Common. The Common was still recognized as

1. A pasture for cows.
2. A play-ground for children.
3. A place for beating carpets.
4. A training ground for the militia.

It had served these purposes, or some of them, for two hundred years, since Blackstone had first turned in his cows among its savins and blackberries and rocks to pick up a scanty living. In modern days it had not been fenced until 1815. After the war with England there was some money left from a popular subscription for fortifying the harbor, which the Virginian dynasties had, in their way, neglected. This money was used for making a wooden fence around the Common. The rails of this fence were hexagonal—two or three inches in diameter, perhaps. If a flat side were on top, as was generally the case, it made a good seat for boys, as they sat on the top rail with their feet on the second. If the corner came uppermost it was not so good. The fence was double—inside the mall and outside. When a muster took place, or Artillery Election, or when the Sacs and Foxes danced on the Common, the space within the inner fence was cleared. Then boys and girls sat on it to witness the sports within, and those taller stood in rows behind.

There cannot be a square yard of the Common on which I have not stood or stepped, and the same could be said of most boys of that time. As for the cows, we saw but little of them. I cannot think that in our time there were ever fifty at once there. They retired to the parts near Charles Street, with which we had less, though much, to do. So did the people who beat carpets. Practically the Common was ours to work our own sweet will upon. On musters, and on the two election days and Independence Day, we shared it with the rest of the town. On those days "Old Reed" would appear with his constable's pole ; but on other days it was ours, and ours only.

Even Mrs. Child, in her *Juvenile Miscellany*, gave the impression that the coasting scene, in which the Latin School boys defied General Gage, began with coasting on the Common. But she was wholly wrong there. In 1775 no boy went out of town to coast on the Common. And the famous embassy which the Latin School boys sent to General Haldimand, to complain that their rights were violated, negotiated about a coast which went down Beacon Street, across Tremont Street, and down School Street, opposite their school. The story was told me by Mr. Robins, the last survivor of the delegation.

Fifty-five years later we coasted on Beacon Street when we dared. But this was in face of the ordinances of the young city. In one of Dr. Jacob Bigelow's funny poems, printed in the *Advertiser* in 1820, he made himself our spokesman :

Mr. Heyward, Mr. Heyward, be a little kinder.
Can't you wink a little bit, or be a little blinder ?
Can't you let us coasting fellows have a little fun ?
Were you born old, or was't your way all childish
    sports to shun ?

Did you ne'er know how slick it is to coast from top to
  bottom ?
And can't we use our ironers and planers, now we've got
  'em ?
Five dollars makes our pas look cross—that's proper bad,
  you know ;
Our youth will soon be gone, alas ! and sooner still the
  snow.

Caleb Heyward was the police officer of the
day.

Practically we went to the Common for
coasting. The smaller boys made a coast on
Park Street mall. But the great coast was
from the foot of Walnut Street, where a well-
marked path runs now, leaving the great elm
on the right as you went down.

This may be my last chance to put on paper
a note of Lord Percy's encampment. His
brigade, in the winter of 1775–76, and perhaps
of the previous year, was encamped in tents, in
a line stretching south-west from the head of
West Street. As the weather grew cold the
tents were doubled, and the space between the
two canvas roofs was filled with straw. The
circles made by such tents and the life in them
showed themselves in a different color of the
grass for a hundred years after Percy's time.
The line is now almost all taken up by what I

may call the highway from the Providence station down town.

As the snow melted, and the elms blossomed, and the grass came, the Common opened itself to every sort of game. We played marbles in holes in the malls. We flew kites everywhere, not troubled, as boys would be now, by trees on the cross-paths, for there were no such trees. The old elm and a large willow by the Frog Pond were the only trees within the pentagon made by the malls and the burial-ground. Kite-flying was, as it is, a science ; and on a fine summer day, with south-west winds, a line of boys would be camped in groups, watching or tending their favorite kites as they hung in the air over Park Street. Occasionally a string would break. It was a matter of honor to save your twine. I remember following my falling kite, with no clue but the direction in which I saw it last, till I found that the twine was lying across a narrow court which opened where the Albion Hotel is now. There were two rows of three-story houses which made the court, and my twine festooned it, supported by the ridge-poles of the roofs on either side. I rang a doorbell, stated my case, and ran up, almost without permission, into the attic. Here I climbed out of the attic window, ran up the roof as *Teddy the Tyler* might have done, and drew in the coveted twine. For the pecuniary value of the twine we cared little ; but it would have been, in a fashion, disgraceful to lose it.

Boats on the Frog Pond were much what they are now. The bottom of the pond was not paved until 1848. There were no frogs, so far as I know, but some small horned pout were left there, for which boys fished occasionally. The curb around the pond was laid in Mr. Quincy's day, in 1823 ; I mean when he was mayor. To provide the stone the last of the boulders on the Common were blasted. In old days, as appears from Sewall, they were plenty ; he blasted enough for the foundations of a barn. I think the old Hancock House was built from such boulders. Among those destroyed was the Wishing Stone. This stood—or so Dr. Shurtleff told me—where two paths now join, a little east of the foot of Walnut Street. If you went round it backward nine times, and repeated the Lord's Prayer backward, what-

ever you wished would come to pass. I once
proposed to the mayor and aldermen to go
round the Frog Pond nine times backward and
wish that the city debt might be reduced fifty
per cent. But they have never had the faith
to try. Mr. Quincy proposed that the Frog
Pond should be called Crescent Lake. But
nobody ever really called it so. I have seen
the name on maps, I think, but it is now forgotten.

Charles Street was new in those days, and the
handsome elms which shade the Charles Street
mall were young trees, just planted, in 1825.
By the building of the mill-dam, about that
time, the water was shut out from the southern
side of Charles Street. There existed a superstition among the boys that law did not
extend to the flat, because it was below high-
water mark. On holidays, therefore, there
would be shaking of props and other games of
mild gambling there, which " Old Reed " did
not permit on the upland. This was, of course,
a ridiculous boyish superstition. In those
days, however, we had a large number of sea-
faring men, who brought with them foreign

customs. Among others was the use of "props," a gambling game which the boys had introduced perfectly innocently as an element in playing marbles. I dare say people played props for money on the dried surface of the Back Bay.

Of all the entertainments of the Common, however, nothing, to our mind, compared with the facilities which the malls gave for driving hoop and for post-offices. The connection of the two may not be understood at first, and I will describe it. When the season for driving hoops came round—for, as Mr. Howells has remarked, such things are regulated by seasons as much as is the coming of apple blossoms— we examined last year's hoops, and, if they had come to grief, Fullum negotiated some arrangements by which we had large hoops from sea-going casks. I see none such now. These hoops were as distinguished in their way as Suñol is to-day in hers. My hoop was named Whitefoot. With these hoops it was our business to carry a daily mail.

The daily mail was made chiefly from small newspapers, which were cut from the leading

columns of larger ones. In an editor's house
we had plenty. The Quebec *Gazette* was specially chosen, because its column head was a
small copy of its larger head, and squares cut
from that column made very good little papers.
With a supply of these folded, we started at
the head of Park Street, two or three of us,
secret as the grave, to leave the day's mail.

No, I will not, after sixty years, tell where
those post-offices were. I have no doubt that
the ashes of the Quebec *Gazette* are now fertil-
izing some of those elms. But one was near
Joy Street, one was in a heart which some landscape gardener had cut in the turf near Spruce
Street, one was half-way along Charles Street.
They were holes in the ground, or *caches* between the roots of trees. At each was a box—
or, in one case, two tight-fitting oyster shells—
which received the mail. From it the yester-
day's mail was taken to the next office.

When the mail-riders with their hoops
arrived at one of these post-offices they threw
themselves negligently upon the ground, as
if tired; but one dug with care for the box
buried below. Of course he found it, unless

some fatal landscape gardener, of whom the Common knew but few, had interfered. When found, the paper or letter from the last office was left here, the sods or stones or sand were replaced, and the cautious mail-riders galloped on. At the end of a winter the chances were worse for finding a mail, or after a long rain or vacation.

There was then no mall on Boylston Street. The burial-ground, with a brick wall, ran close to the street, and there was no sidewalk on that side, so that we generally crossed by the line of Percy's encampments. And to all boys, I imagine, that little corner where the deer park is was comparatively little known.

It is, however, a waste of honest paper to be telling of such trifles about the Common, when its great importance was as a training field, or for holidays, as one may read in Sewall's Diary, and in the old votes of the town. There were four holidays in the year—'Lection proper, Artillery Election (generally called 'Tillery 'Lection), the Fourth of July (called Independence Day, I think, more than it is now), and, in October, Muster, or the Fall

Training. By good luck, of course, Lafayette might come along, or General Jackson, or the Sacs and Foxes might dance, but these could not be expected.

Since I first printed these notes, a dozen letters have informed me that people have forgotten who the Sacs and Foxes were. The Sacs and Foxes were an important branch of the great Chippewa race, and they lived in Northern Illinois, in the region which is now called Wisconsin, and farther north. Under the lead of Black Hawk, a famous fighter, and Keokuk, they made head against the settlers in that region, and their power was only broken by a military campaign, in which the United States Army repressed them. It was then thought that it would be a good thing for the Indians of the frontier to show them the greatness of the cities of the East. So Black Hawk and Keokuk and some other braves were brought round from Washington to the Northern cities, and they appeared in Boston in the autumn of 1838. Governor Everett received them at the State House, and they made speeches to him, and he made speeches to them. After this they danced a war dance, or what was called such, on the Common, to the great delight of all the people of the neighborhood.

And alas! by a utilitarian revolution, in 1831, the real old Election Day was changed from the last Wednesday in May to the 1st of January. When my father confessed to me that he had himself voted for the change in the constitution of Massachusetts, I think he did it with a certain shame. I was at that time nine years old, so that I could not rebuke him as the vote seemed to require. But he knew, and they all knew, that if the vote had been submitted to the children of Boston, no such innovation would have been made.

Unlearned readers, unhappily not born in Massachusetts, must be informed that, under the first charter of Massachusetts, "yearly once in the year forever after, namely, the last Wednesday in Easter term yearly, the Governor, deputy governor, and assistants of the said company, and all other officers shall be in the General Court duly chosen." Under the charter of the province, given by William and

Mary, the last Wednesday in May was fixed for the beginning of the political year; and when the constitution of the State was made, in 1779, the same date was retained. The General Court met—that is the name to this day of the legislature of Massachusetts; in the first charter it meant what we should call a stockholders' meeting. In old days the General Court elected the Governor on this day; so Winthrop, Dudley, and all the early governors were elected. Under the constitution the election returns were examined on this day, and perhaps reported on. Anyway the legislature met, referred them to a committee, and, under escort of the Cadets, who were the Governor's guard, they marched to the Old South Meeting House to hear the election sermon.

With these intricacies of government I need not say the boys of Boston had nothing to do. What was truly important was the festivity, principally on the Common, of Election Day. Early in the morning, perhaps even Tuesday evening, hucksters of every kind began to put up their tables, tents, and stalls on each side of the Tremont Street mall, and, to a less extent, on the other malls. On the Common itself a mysterious man—in a mysterious octagonal house painted green and red, as I remember—displayed camera views of the scene. Of these I speak from hearsay, for I never had money enough to pay for admission to this secret chamber.

I found in Hawthorne's "English Note-book" some curious bits of information about fairs in England, which reminded me, queerly, of some of these customs of our New England holidays on the Common.

To prepare for these festivities every child in Boston expected "'Lection money." 'Lection money was money given specifically to be spent on the Common on Election Day. The day before Election my mother sent Fullum to the office for three or four dollars' worth of silver; and she knew that all her train of vassals, so far as they could pretend to be children, would expect "'Lection money" from her. First, she had her own children, to whom she gave twelve and a half cents each. There was a considerable number of nephews and nieces who might or might not look in; but if they did, each of them was also sure to have a "ninepence," which was the name given to the Spanish piece which was half a "quarter dollar." American silver coinage was still very rare.

It may be of use to young orators, getting ready to speak on the silver question, to know that when, in 1652, the colony of Massachusetts Bay assumed the royal privilege of the mint and coined its own silver, the leaders thought they could keep this silver at home by making the coin two-thirds the weight of the king's silver. The Massachusetts shilling, therefore, was two-thirds the weight of the English shilling. Six shillings went to the Spanish dollar. It proved that Spanish coin became very largely the currency of the colonies, and so of the States, for long years after independence. We took the Spanish dollar for our unit when we made a national currency. Twelve and a half cents of that currency, the old Spanish real piece, became worth ninepence in the Massachusetts standard ; and fourpence-halfpenny and ninepence,

"IF I HAPPENED TO MEET AN UNCLE, HE WOULD ASK ME IF
I DID NOT WANT SOME ELECTION MONEY."—*Page* 103.

the half-real and real of the early time, were the coins most familiar to children. The "piece of eight" in "Robinson Crusoe" is a dollar piece, amounting to eight of our ninepences. Old-fashioned New Englanders will to this hour speak of seventy-five cents as "four-and-sixpence," or of thirty-seven and a half cents as "two-and-threepence." These measures are in pine-tree currency.

To come back to Election money. Other retainers expected it. There were families of black children, who never appeared at any other time, who would come in with smiling faces and make a little call. Mother would give each one his or her ninepence. On the other hand, if in the street I happened to meet an uncle, he would ask me if I did not want some Election money, and produce his ninepence. I never heard of "tipping" in any other connection, except when a boy held water for a horse as you rode anywhere ; then you always gave him a bit of silver or a few cents.

Thus provided with the sinews of war, we went up on the Common with such company

as might have happened along—girls with
girls, and boys with boys. The buying and
selling were confined almost wholly to things
to eat and drink ; though there is a bad story
told of me, that, having gone out with a
quarter of a dollar one morning, I spent the
whole of it for a leather purse, into which,
for the rest of the day, I had nothing to
put. This is my experience of Ben Franklin's
whistle. Certain things were sold there which
we never saw sold anywhere else, and which
we should never have thought of buying anywhere else. Boston was then in active trade
with the West Indies, more than it is now.
You could not bring bananas in the long
schooner voyages of that time, but we had
cocoanuts in plenty, and occasionally a bit of
sugarcane. I do not think I had ever seen a
banana when I was twenty years old.

It happened oddly enough that tamarinds,
in the curious "original packages," were
always for sale, and dates, of which we did
not see much on other occasions. At home we
never had oysters, I believe because my father
did not like them ; but on the Common we could

buy two oysters for a cent, and we ate them
with rapture. To this day I doubt if a raw
oyster is ever as good, as it was when eaten
under the trees of Park Street mall, with vine-
gar and pepper and salt *ad libitum*, and this
in May ! Candy of all kinds then known was
for sale, but the kinds were limited. There
was one manufactured form which, I am sorry
to say, has died out. One or two dealers sold
large medals of checkerberry stamped with a
head. Whom this originally represented I do
not know, but very early we all said it was
John Endicott, because he was the first Governor of Massachusetts Bay, and we called
them "John Endicotts." I advertised in a
newspaper, a few years ago, for anybody who
knew how to make these things, but I had no
answer. You would see sailor-looking men eating lobsters, but those we were quite sure of at
home. Ginger beer and spruce beer were sold
from funny little wheelbarrows, which had
attractive pictures of the bottles throwing out
the corks by their own improvised action.
You might have a glass of spruce beer for two
cents, and, to boys as impecunious as most of

us were, the dealers would sell half a glass for one cent. Why we did not all die of the trash which we ate and drank on such occasions I do not know. But we are alive, a good many of us, to tell the story to this hour.

In all this we had little thought or care for the election itself. Independence Day passed in much the same fashion. I remember, as I returned home from the Common, having expended every cent of my money, one Independence Day, I saw a procession of children going into Park Street Church. To see a church open on a week-day was itself extraordinary. To see children going in procession into a church was more extraordinary. With a disposition to find out what was going on I followed in the train, and went into the gallery. We were not orthodox at our house, but I had been in that meeting-house before. I soon perceived that this was a Sunday-school entertainment, at which I remained as long as seemed pleasing to me, and then retired. I have no recollection of anything that passed there, but, by putting the dates together, I am fond of believing that then and there I heard

Dr. Smith's national song, "My Country, 'tis of Thee," sung for the first time that it was ever sung in public. Possibly my untrained voice joined in the enthusiasm of the strain.

It was at one of the first of the elections after the anniversary had been changed to January that an event took place which made quite a mark in the local history, and to which boys attached immense importance. Governor Lincoln had been escorted to the Old South Meeting-House by the Cadets, whose force was not large at that time. The escort had opened to the right and the left for the civic procession to pass in, and then, instead of following them, had repaired to the Exchange Coffee-House for refreshment. The commander had left a messenger, who was to inform him when the sermon approached its close, so that he might be ready with the escort at the door of the church to go back with the Governor to the State House. Unfortunately the preacher wound up too suddenly, the hymn which followed the sermon was too short, and when the Governor, who was the prince of punctilio in such matters, came, with the council and the legislature, to the door, there was no escort. Governor Lincoln walked up Winter Street with the gentlemen of his personal staff, but without any Cadets. The colonel of the Cadets arrived at the church a minute too late. He put his men at double quick, and they fairly ran up Bromfield Street, and came to the corner of the Common in time to meet the Governor, and presented arms. But the Governor declined to recognize his escort, and proceeded on the sidewalk to the State House or his lodging-house, with the melancholy Cadets following as they might. A court-martial ensued, of which the proceedings are in print ; and military circles and the circles of school-boys were highly excited about it. It was one of the fortunate events of my early life that I stumbled on the Governor and his staff as they walked up Winter Street on that fatal occasion.

On the evening of Independence Day there was sometimes a display of fireworks on the Common ; but the science of pyrotechnics was then but little advanced in America, and there was much more waiting than there was exhibition. My recollections of these displays are of our always leaving to go home, tired out, before the successful pieces were shown. To the boys and girls of to-day it will be interesting to know that the pieces were set up either for spectators who stood on the hill and looked down toward St. Paul's Church, or near the foot of Walnut Street for groups of spectators below, who were to look up to them there. The entire absence of trees from the Common inside the malls, enabled those in charge to make the stages for the fireworks just where they pleased.

The military system of the State in those days required two annual parades, in which every militiaman should appear with his gun and other equipments. It is by a comparatively modern arrangement that the State or the United States furnishes the arms for the militia. Under the simpler arrangements of the colony, and of the State at the beginning, every man who considered himself a man was obliged to have a gun, a cartridge-box, a belt, a "primer," and the other necessaries for an infantry soldier. We therefore had, in the attic, Fullum's gun, cartridge-box, and primer, which made good properties, in any theatricals which required the presence of an army. My father had been a member of the New England Guards, but his gun was kept in their armory.

These arms the militiaman bought with his own money, and he must produce them once a year for inspection. I believe that they were shown at a certain spring meeting, to which comparatively little attention was given by boys. But in the autumn, every man between the ages of eighteen and forty-five, unless he were on the list of "exempts," had to appear in person, with his gun, belt, and cartridge-box, to show that the commonwealth had him as a soldier, and that he knew something of the art of arms.

Young men who had a real interest in the military art did as they do now. They volunteered into what were called the "volunteer companies," or sometimes the "flank companies." These companies had uniforms, had generally their own separate charters as fusileers, rangers, light infantry, or guards; they were proud of their history; the State or somebody provided them with armories—generally over Faneuil Hall—and they had frequent parades, while they had sufficient instruction for keeping up their military discipline. All this was precisely as uniformed militia companies exist to-day. But now the other militiamen are simply on a certain register, which they never see and of which they know nothing—though they are counted to the credit of Massachusetts in the quota which exists at Washington. Then, the militiaman had to appear and show himself; and this he did at the annual training. A man knew to what company he belonged. He was notified that he must attend at a certain place on the morning of the Fall Muster; he did attend there, and thence he marched to the Common for the fall training.

The military zeal of the War of 1812 had not wholly died out, but there was beginning to be a suspicion that the conditions of peace were such that it was not necessary for every man to be trained to arms. A certain ridicule, therefore, attached itself to what was called the "militia" in distinction from the "vol-

unteer companies.'' Occasionally a militia
company, under spirited lead, tried to distin-
guish itself by its drill, but this seldom happened. Old Boston people will remember a
joke of that time about the Berry Street
Rangers. The particular company, which met
in front of Dr. Channing's church in Berry
Street, chose one year as their captain a gentleman who, they thought, would let them off
lightly. But he interested himself at once in
bringing up the company's equipment and
drill, and gave them the name of the Berry
Street Rangers, so that for some years we
heard of their exploits in one way or another.

The interest among young men which now
goes largely to the keeping up of military companies was then expended in great measure
on the volunteer fire department. Still, when
the fall training came, the interest of the boys
was naturally in the companies which were in
uniform ; and when the parade was formed on
the Common these companies always held the
right of the line, either by courtesy or because
they were entitled to it by law. According as
the major-general commanding had more or

less enthusiasm there would or would not be a sham fight. The whole Common was cleared for these exercises. Of course a considerable detail of melancholy sentinels was required to keep the boys from running in, and the principal fights, sham or real, on these occasions, were their contests with these sentinels. But as the army to be reviewed really amounted to one-fifth of the men of Boston, even after this large detail of sentries, there would be a considerable force in the field. It seems to me that the line always extended, with its back to the Tremont Street mall, for the whole length of that mall. The reviewing officers would pass it, as in any review to-day, and then the sham fight would begin. We boys, sitting on the fence, criticised the manœuvres of this Waterloo, with such information on tactics as we had got from reading Botta's " History of the American Revolution " or Cæsar's " Commentaries on the War with Gaul." I recollect a sham fight in which the hill—still fortified, as I have said—was defended against an attack. It appears to me, however, that the attacks were generally made by the whole force against an unseen enemy. This mode of fighting has its advantages. Practically, however, after the Rangers had been thrown out as skirmishers, and the different companies had moved backward and forward across the Common, at about five in the afternoon the whole line was formed again, and a discharge of blank cartridges began, which lasted till all the cartridges of all the soldiers were burned up. I say all the cartridges, but we would solicit Fullum to slip one or more cartridges into his pocket instead of firing them off, and on rare occasions he succeeded in doing this. Then there were superstitions that individual soldiers were afraid to burn their cartridges, and dropped them surreptitiously on the grass, so that, the next morning, we always went over to the Common to see if we could not find some of these. I cannot recollect that any boy ever did. The actual presence of war, as it showed itself in this discharge of powder, was of course very attractive, and "Muster" had a certain value which belonged to none of the other holidays of the year.

There was great antipathy in the ruling cir-

cles at our house to boating, in any of the
forms then pursued in the harbor. On the
other hand, my father and mother were both
country bred, and, as I believe I have said,
my mother was very fond of flowers. As
soon as spring opened, in the earlier days,
father and mother went to drive very often
on Thursday and Saturday afternoons. This
drive was taken in the chaise, and, for the purpose of the ride, a little seat was fitted in,
which was in fact a trunk, in which mother
brought home any wild flowers which she
picked. On this trunk one of "us four"
went, in a regular order laid down by the
Medes and Persians. This entertainment of
a holiday was one of the great joys of my
early life. But, for the half-holidays which
were not thus provided for, my brother and
I took care by using "the means which God
and nature put into our hands." That is to
say, we walked out of town to such woodland
generally as we had not explored before, until
we were personally acquainted with the whole
country for a circle of five miles' radius around
the State House.

An enterprising English surveyor named
John G. Hales had lived in Boston long enough
to make a good working map of the suburbs
of Boston. He printed a little book, still
known to the curious, on that region. He
was rather in advance of the times, I suppose,
and when he succumbed to adversity, my
father bought from him all the plates and
drawings of his different maps. Among these
was the map of Boston and vicinity, which
is still a good map, and is still regularly
stolen from by anybody who wants to pub-
lish such a map, without much regard to
any copyright which existed in the original
surveys. Two or three times new editions of
this map were published, and in such a case
"we four" generally had more or less to do
with the painting of the different towns, so
that their lines might be the better designated.
It thus happens that at this moment I could
pass, with some credit, any competitive examination which should turn on the township
lines of the various towns within fifteen miles
of Boston.

But the personal knowledge, gained by

tramping through the interior circle of such towns, was worth much more than the painting. The Hales map indicated the several pieces of scrub woodland which were then left, and to such woodland we boys regularly repaired. I need not say that such expeditions were encouraged at home. Whenever we chose to undertake one two cents were added to our allowance for the purchase of luncheon.

We always kept for such expeditions what were known as phosphorus-boxes, which were the first steps in the progress that has put the tinder-boxes of that day entirely out of sight. Most of the young people of the present day have not so much as seen a tinder-box, and I do not know where I should go to buy one. But, in the working of the household, the tinder-box was the one resource for getting a light. We boys, however, with the lavishness of boys, used to buy at the apothecary's phosphorus-boxes, which were then coming in. We had to pay twenty-five cents for one such box. These boxes were made in Germany; they were of red paper, little cylinders about four inches high and an inch in diameter. You could carry one, and were meant to carry it, in your breast pocket. In the bottom was a little bottle which contained asbestos soaked with sulphuric acid, and in the top were about a hundred matches, made, I think, from chlorate of potash. One of these you put into the bottle, and pulled it out aflame. We never should have thought of taking one of these walks without a phosphorus-box. When we arrived at the woodland sought we invariably made a little fire. We never cooked anything that I remember, but this love of fire is one of the earlier barbarisms of the human race which dies out latest. I suppose if it had been the middle of the hottest day in August we should have made a fire.

So soon as the morning session of school was over, in the summer or autumn months, if it were a half-holiday, we would start on one of these rambles. Sometimes, if the walk were not to a great distance, we invited, or permitted, the two girls to come with us. We had a tin box for plants, and always brought home what seemed new or pretty. On rare occasions, when we had made up a larger party, we took the "truck" with us, that we might treat any weaker member of the party to a ride. The truck was quite a fashionable plaything at that time ; I do not see it much now, excepting in the hands of boys who have to use it for freight. But in those days boys rode on trucks a good deal. A truck was a pair of wooden wheels on a stout axle—generally not stout enough—with two thills, in which the boy harnessed himself by the simple process of taking hold of them with his hands. If he chose to be jaunty he had twine reins passed under his arms, that the person who sat on the seat of the truck might pretend to be driving.

When, in 1833, the Worcester Railroad was opened, this walking gave way, for a family as largely interested in that railroad as we were, to excursions out of town to the point where the walk was to begin. The line to West Newton was opened to the public on the 7th of April, 1833, but from the day when the *Meteor*, which was the first locomotive engine in New England, ran on her trial trip, we two boys were generally present at the railroad, on every half-holiday, to take our chances for a ride out upon one of the experimental trips. We knew the engine-drivers and the men who were not yet called conductors, and they knew us. My father was the president of the road, and we thought we did pretty much as we chose. The engine-drivers would let us ride with them on the engine, and I, for one, got my first lessons in the business of driving an engine on those excursions. But so soon as the road was open to passengers, these rides on the engine dropped off, perhaps were prohibited. Still we went to Newton as often as we could in the train, and afterwards to Needham. There were varied cars in those days, some of them open, like our open horse-cars of to-day, and all of them entered from the side, as in England up to the present time. After this date our long walks out of town naturally ceased. Nothing was more common in our household than for the whole family to go out to Brighton or to Newton, and, with babies and all, to establish ourselves in some grove, where we spent the afternoon very much as

God meant we should spend it, I suppose; returning late in the evening with such spoils of wild flowers as the season permitted.

More methodical excursions out of town took forms quite different from what they would take to-day. At our house the custom was to deride canals in proportion as we glorified railroads. All the same, I think in the summer of 1826—still recollected as the hottest summer which has been known in this century in New England—it was announced one day that we were going to Chelmsford, and that we were going by the canal. I have no recollection of the method by which we struck the Middlesex Canal; I suppose that we had to drive to East Cambridge and take the *General Sullivan* there. The *General Sullivan* was what was known, I think, as a packet-boat, which carried passengers daily from Boston to the Merrimac River, where the name "Lowell" had just then been given to a part of the township of Chelmsford. Mr. Samuel Batchelder, the distinguished engineer and manufacturer, to whom New England owes so much, was one of my father's most intimate friends. He was engaged in some of the first works at Lowell, and, by way of escape from the heat, father had arranged that the whole family should go down to the tavern at Chelmsford and spend a few days.

The present generation does not know it, but travelling on a canal is one of the most charming ways of travelling. We are all so crazy to go fifty miles an hour that we feel as if we had lost something when we only go five miles an hour. All the same, to sit on the deck of a boat and see the country slide by you, without the slightest jar, without a cinder or a speck of dust, is one of the exquisite luxuries. The difficulty about speed is much reduced if you will remember, with Red Jacket, that "you have all the time there is." And I have found it not impossible to imagine that the distance over which I am going is ten times as great as in fact the statistical book would make it. Simply I think a man may get as much pleasure out of a journey to Lowell on a canal which is thirty miles long as he may out of a journey of three hundred miles by rail between Albany and Buffalo.

But this leads into metaphysical considerations which do not belong to the boyhood of New England.

What did belong to it was a series of very early reminiscences which have clung to me when more important things have been forgotten. Fullum, of course, was of the party. He would spring from the deck of the *General Sullivan* upon the tow-path, and walk along collecting wild flowers, or perhaps even more active game. I have never forgotten my terror lest Fullum should be left by the boat and should never return. When he did return from one of these forays he brought with him for us children a very little toad, the first I had ever seen. My mother put him in her thimble he was so small. Not long after we heard that a delicate friend of hers had taken cold because she put on her thimble when it was damp. With a child's facility, I always associated the two thimbles with each other; and I think I may say I never see a little toad now, without imagining that he is carrying the seeds of catarrh or influenza to some delicate invalid.

We stayed at the old tavern on the Merri-mac, which, I suppose, was long ago pulled down. A story of that time tells how Mr. Isaac P. Davis, who was, I think, one of the proprietors of the locks and canals which made Lowell, went to this same hotel with a party, and inquired what they were to have for dinner. The keeper said that a good salmon had come up the river the night before, and he proposed to serve him—with which answer Mr. Davis was well pleased. Later in the morning he said he should like to see the salmon. But the man only expressed his amazement at such folly on the part of a Boston man. "You don't suppose I would take him out of the water, do you ? He is in the water at the foot of the falls, and has been there since last night. When it is time to cook him, I shall go out and catch him."

CHAPTER VI.

SOCIAL RELATIONS.

I AM painfully aware that, to the diligent reader of the last two parts of this historical study, it may seem as if the boys described were a sort of Robinson Crusoe and man Friday who lived alone on their happy island. I feel as if I had spoken as though there were an occasional invasion of savages or Spaniards, but that practically we had little to do with the outside world. This is by no means true, and I will now try to give some idea of the social conditions which surrounded boyhood in Boston in the years between 1826 and 1837. For we were "in the swim," as the current expression puts it, and no countenance would have been given to us, either in any shyness or for any arrogance which kept us out of it.

I have already said that, while on the most cordial terms with our school companions, it

seemed as if we left them in another world as
soon as school was over. As I have said, I
think the reason was that most of the fathers
of the other boys were in mercantile pursuits,
and the boys' business, therefore, called them
quite regularly to the wharves to inspect the
large foreign trade of Boston. As it happened,
our father was in other affairs, and, as naturally, these attracted us.

In an old New England family, church-
going, of course, was an element which had a
great deal to do with social life. I was carried
to "meeting" on the fourth Sunday after I
was born, and was christened at the same time
with two or three other children. I afterwards
knew their names. They were in families with
whom we were well acquainted, and to this
hour that mystic tie seems to form a relationship between me and them and their children.
I have to this moment a little bit of yellow
paper which is, I fancy, the first document but
one among the memoirs which form my biog-
raphy. It is the bill of the "stable man" who
sent his carriage on this occasion. "For carrying three to meeting, sixty cents." My poor

nine or ten pounds of avoirdupois went as nothing to the hack-driver, and no estimate is made of the cost to him or to the community of the carrying to "meeting" of the person who was, as I must still say, the most important individual in the transaction.

In those days children were taken to church for regular attendance very early. I do not see any children in my own church who are as young as those who went or were taken then. On our annual visits to Westhampton we were always interested because the young mothers carried their babies to "meeting," at all ages. They did not like, I suppose, to stay at home when all the men "went to meeting," and accordingly they went with the children. If a baby cried the mother got up, carried it out, and sat on the steps of the meeting-house until the ebullition of feeling was over, when she returned. But this was rather edifying as an interesting curiosity to us Boston children. No babies were carried to Brattle Street Church except for baptism ; but as soon as the children could walk, and be relied upon not to cry, I should think the custom began.

Such reliance was sometimes misplaced. I am so unfortunate that I do not remember ever hearing Dr. Channing preach ; but it is among the disgraceful records of my life that once, when my mother thought she would hear him, and, because Brattle Street Church was being painted, went to Federal Street, she took me with her. She sat with friends, far forward in the broad aisle, and I, dissatisfied with the interior arrangements of the church, I suppose —probably dissatisfied because I was not where I was used to be on Sunday—wept with such loud acclaim that in the middle of the service she was obliged to rise and take me out of the church. I think it was the last experiment of the sort that she tried. In fact, we were very loyal to our church. I think all people were loyal to the churches they went to. And to such unfortunate loyalty I owe it that, while I knew Dr. Channing personally, and he was very kind to me as a boy, I never had the pleasure of hearing him preach, excepting on the occasion named, although I was twenty years old when he died. I have, more than once, heard him speak, but never from the pulpit.

We "went to meeting" morning and afternoon always, and so, I am apt to think, did
all respectable people ; certainly in the earlier
part of those years. I know that I never
observed any distinction between the size of
the congregation in the afternoon and that of
the morning. I know that any person who
had been seen driving out of town on Sunday,
either in the morning or in the afternoon,
would have lost credit in the community. Frequently Mr. Palfrey, the minister, would say,
at the end of the morning's sermon, " I shall
continue this subject in the afternoon." He
did so with the perfect understanding that he
would have the same hearers. I wonder, in
passing, whether that phrase "my hearers"
is as familiar to young people now as it was
then. It was a bit of pulpit slang, such as
one never hears in a lecture-room or in a
political meeting. The people, instead of
being addressed as "you" or as "friends,"
or as "members of the Church of Christ,"
were spoken to as "hearers." I doubt if I
ever hear that word now without giving it a
certain ecclesiastical connection.

It was a wonder to me then, and has been ever since, why the hour and a quarter spent in "meeting" of a Sunday morning seemed as long as the four hours spent in school every other morning. I was early aware of the curiously interesting fact, which nobody ever explained to me, that the afternoon service was ten minutes shorter than the morning service; but why that hour and five minutes should seem as long as the three hours spent in school of an afternoon I have never known, and do not know now. Besides these two services, we had the Sunday-school. It seems to me it was always after the afternoon service; I know it was in the earlier days. A Sunday-school then was a very different thing from what it is now. Then you were expected to learn something, and you did. For my own part, I have often said, and I think it is true, that fully one-half of the important information which I now have with regard to the Scriptural history of mankind—with regard to the history of the Jews, for instance, or the travels of Paul right and left, or anything else which can be called the intellectual side of the Bible—was acquired in Brattle Street Sunday-school before I was thirteen years old. We had little books which contained facts on these subjects. We had to study these books as we did any other school-books, and we recited from them as we recited any other lesson. I do not think there was much said or thought about making Sunday-school agreeable to the children. We were told to go, and we went; we were told to learn a lesson, and we learned it. As I observe Sunday-schools now, this has been driven out, and driven out, I believe, by the pressure of the week-day school system—a pressure which I am fighting against in every quarter without success. For myself, I liked to go where my brother and sisters went. They went to the Sunday-school, so I expressed a wish to go.

Pupils were received there then, on the 1st of January, and on the first Sunday of the year 1827 I presented myself with the rest. But it proved that the rule of the school was that no one should be admitted before he was six. I suppose they did not want children who could not read. I could read as well as I can now, and was disgusted, therefore, when I was rejected on examination. I rather think I was the only child in New England who was ever told that he must not go to Sunday-school. But I was sent away on the ground that I was not six years old. I went home with the others, saying, "It is a pretty way to hear a fellow say his catechism by asking him, 'How old are you?' 'How old are you?' 'How old are you?'" And I was not permitted to go for the next year. I had already taken the first steps in the catechism. I had learned in words what I probably knew already—all, indeed, that is very important to learn in the business of theology.

Such was going to meeting on Sunday. I suppose the sons of Episcopalian families spoke of "going to church," but we did not in my earlier childhood. I make the note here, however, for the benefit of "Notes and Queries," that, in Boston, the meeting-houses were always called churches from the very beginning. I think they were not in other parts of Massachusetts. In Hales's map of this neighborhood, of the date of 1826, you will see "Rev. Mr. Gray's M. H.," "Rev. Mr. Gile's M. H.," meaning "meeting-house" in each instance.

Of week-day exercises connected with churches Boston knew almost nothing, not even in Evangelical circles. The fact was known that there was a chandelier in the Old South Church, but I do not think the chandelier was often lighted. When Park Street Church was built, as a sort of banner of a new dispensation for latitudinarian Boston, it had arrangements for lighting the church for an evening service. But this was all a heresy to the old Boston Puritan, whether he were Evangelical or Unitarian.

For the original theory of the Puritans is that the family is the church, and that each family is a church. The father of each family is a priest, and is competent to carry on worship. Accordingly he does carry on worship in the morning and in the evening ; and any proposal for an evening service anywhere else was regarded by the old Puritans as being, to a certain extent, an innovation, because it broke up that family worship which was so essential in their plan. I think that in every family of which I had any acquaintance the forms of family worship were maintained in this earlier period; every morning certainly, and probably every evening. When, therefore, the religion of Connecticut was introduced into Boston by the building of Park Street Church, and by the arrival of my children's great-grandfather, Lyman Beecher, and the custom of an occasional evening service on Sunday or on a weekday came with it, it was considered as an entire innovation by old-fashioned Boston. It was quite as much an innovation as calling an Episcopal minister a "rector" is now to old-fashioned Episcopalians, or as having lighted candles in the daytime would be at Trinity. To the last moment of its conscious existence the West Church was never arranged for evening service; and at this moment you will find, in old Boston families, the habit of going to visit one another on Sunday evening, but not of going to church. Where people go to church steadily on Sunday evening you may generally guess they are not of old Boston blood.

In the interior of the State, as at my grandfather's, for example, the observance of "the
Sabbath" stopped at sunset. For instance, we
watched at his house for the sun to go down
on Sunday afternoon, and then brought out
our little cannons and fired a *feu de joie* in
honor of its departure. We then played blind-
man's-buff all Sunday evening, and this in the
parsonage of a stiff Calvinistic minister. No
such excesses as this would have been permitted in Boston. But gradually Sunday
evening concerts came in, if only they were
religious concerts ; and the Handel and Haydn
Society, I think, would hardly have been in
existence now but for the midway opportunity
which Sunday evening gave for their performances. The theatres, on the other hand, were
compelled to be closed on Saturday evening
and on Sunday, until a period later than that
I am describing, when some of the more enterprising managers defied the State and the city,
and our statutes were changed so that performances on Saturday evening were possible.
After they had gained the point as a matter of
right I think they generally found it more

convenient to have the performances of Saturday in the afternoon. Our present statute, which defines the Lord's Day as from midnight to midnight, is as late as 1844. Before that time there were certain restrictions on Saturday evening, such as the theatrical licenses indicated.

Perhaps the great central day which gave distinction and hope to the duty of going to meeting was the proclamation of Thanksgiving. Let me describe a scene in Brattle Street Meeting-House.

The time is the middle of November, on a Sunday morning. A boy of four years old, who has the fortunate privilege of sitting on the cross-seat of the pew, is the person who describes, after sixty-six years, what he remembers. Be it understood by architectural readers that Brattle Street Meeting-House was a fine old church in Boston, built after the best traditions of Wren's churches in London. It has been well said that in the social life of London in the days of Wren there were reasons for the high walls, as they might be called, which in those churches concealed the wor-

shippers in one pew from those in the next.
Whatever was the reason, such high pew walls
were the effect. The little boy, whose self and
successor is now trying to reproduce him,
could sleep, if he chose, extended on the cross-
seat with his head in his mother's lap, while
she listened to the minister. I will not say
that on this particular day he, or I, had been
asleep. What is important to the present
business is that she whispers to him that he
had better listen now, for the minister is going
to read the proclamation. The boy stands up
on his seat, and with that delight with which
even conservative childhood sees any custom
defied watches with rapture Mr. Palfrey
unfolding the large paper sheet, which might
have been a large newspaper, and sees the
sheet cover even the pulpit Bible.

Mr. Palfrey is a young man of thirty or
thereabouts, who is afterwards to be the distinguished Dr. Palfrey, a leader of the Anti-
Slavery opinion of Massachusetts. He reads
the Governor's proclamation with sense and
feeling, so that even a child follows along,
about the taking care of the poor, the happi-

ness of home, but specially about the success of the fisheries. It is only in the latest times that any Massachusetts Governor is so disloyal to that ocean from whose breasts she has drawn her life that he fails to mention The Fisheries in his proclamation. But home, poor people, fisheries, and all sink into their own insignificance when with resonant voice the minister ends—with the grand words :

Given in the Council Chamber at Boston, in the year of our Lord, 1826, and of the Independence of the United States the fiftieth.

LEVI LINCOLN, *Governor.*

This fine relationship between "Thanksgiving Day" and "Independence Day," of which the glories, six months ago, are a certain hazy dream, is not lost upon the child. And then follow the words, most grand in all rituals :

By his Excellency the Governor, with the advice and consent of the Council.

EDWARD D. BANGS, *Secretary.*

GOD SAVE THE COMMONWEALTH OF MASSACHUSETTS!

That words so inspiring, pronounced with such a clarion voice, should be uttered in a church on Sunday—this was indeed something to fill high the cup of wild, intoxicating joy. That Edward D. Bangs, the secretary, should be sitting himself, watching, as it were, his own petard, on the other side of the aisle, with his finger resting on his right ear, in a peculiar manner such as was unknown to others—he clad in a brown coat with a velvet collar—that he should see and hear all this unmoved—this added to the grandeur and solemnity and high dignity of the whole. The minister said that, in accordance with the instructions of the Executive, the church would be open on Thanksgiving Day, and that, before that day —namely, on the next Sunday—a contribution would be taken for the poor. The boy asked his mother if he might bring some money— and was told that he should have a fo'pence for the occasion. "Fo'pence" in the language of the time meant fourpence-halfpenny of the currency of New England. But New England, though she coined threepences with her own pine tree, never coined fourpence-ha'-penny pieces. She used instead the half-real of the Spanish coinage. The boy was to put

in the box, and did put in for many years at
Thanksgiving, one of these coins, small to
kings, but almost the largest known in familiar
use to children.

Passing by the contribution, and the vague
ideas which the children had of the immense
results to be obtained by the distribution of
their wealth among the poor, I will come
directly to Thanksgiving Day itself. Had we
children been asked what we expected on
Thanksgiving Day we should have clapped
our hands and said that we expected a good
dinner. As we had a good dinner every day
of our lives this answer shows simply that
children respect symbols and types. And
indeed there were certain peculiarities in the
Thanksgiving dinner which there were not on
common days. For instance, there was always
a great deal of talk about the Marlborough
pies or the Marlborough pudding. To this
hour, in any old and well-regulated family in
New England, you will find there is a traditional method of making the Marlborough
pie, which is a sort of lemon pie, and each
good housekeeper thinks that her grandmother

left a better receipt for Marlborough pie than anybody else did. We had Marlborough pies at other times, but we were sure to have them on Thanksgiving Day ; and it ought to be said that there was no other day on which we had four kinds of pies on the table and plum pudding beside, not to say chicken pie. In those early days ice creams or sherbets or any of the kickshaws of that variety would have been spurned from a Thanksgiving dinner.

Every human being went to "meeting" on the morning of Thanksgiving Day, the boy of four years included. At that age he did not know that the sermon was, or might be, political. Still an attentive ear might catch words from the pulpit which would not have been heard on Sunday. It was when all parties came home from "meeting" that the real festival began. Not but what frequent visits to the kitchen the day before had familiarized even Young Boston with the gigantic scale on which things were conducted. For it was the business of the kitchen, not simply to supply the feast in that house, but the other feasts in the houses of feudal dependents of different colors, who would render themselves for their pies and their chickens.

The hours absolutely without parallel in the year were the two hours between twelve and two. We were in our best clothes and it was Thanksgiving Day. We therefore did not do what we should have done on other days, and we were the least bit bored by the change. On other days we should have gone and coasted had the snow fallen; or we should have gone into the "garret" and fought an imaginary battle of Salamis on the floats. But this was Thanksgiving Day, and we therefore went into the best parlor, not very often opened, and entertained ourselves, or entertained each other, by looking at picture-books which we could not always see. The Hogarths were out, the illustrated books of travel, the handsome annuals which were rather too fine for our hands at other periods. We were in the position of the boy and girl invited to a party where they know nobody, standing in a corner and pretending to be interested by photographs. But before a great while the cousins would begin to arrive, and then all would be well.   The cousins also were in their best clothes, to which we were not accustomed.   But if we could show them the Hogarths, or they could tell us some experience of theirs in private theatricals, then the joys of society began.   And at two the party, larger than we ever saw it at any other time, went into the back parlor, where the large table was set.   Observe that this large table never appeared, unless the club met with my father, except on Thanksgiving Day.   Christmas Day, as a holiday of this sort, was absolutely unknown in this Puritan family.

There would be a side-table for the children at which the oldest cousin in a manner presided, with his very funny stories, with his very exciting lore about the new life on which he was entering, either in the first class at the Latin School or possibly after he had left the Latin School.   Occasionally the revelry at the side-table became so loud that it had to be suppressed by a word from the elders.   At the elders' table great talk about genealogy : whether Gib Atkins did or did not leave a particular bit of land to certain successors who now own it; whether the Picos and the Robbs were on good terms after the marriage of one of them to another. I will say, in passing, that, as we grew older, we children had the wit to introduce these subjects for the purpose of seeing the mad rage with which different aged cousins advanced to the attack, as a bull might to a red flag.

It may readily be imagined that, with twenty or thirty guests and the innumerable courses, the company, who were indeed in no haste, sat a good while at the table. This was one of the marvels to us children, that it was possible to be at dinner two hours. There was no desire to slip down from the chair and go off to play. There was no soup dreamed of, and I think, to this day, that there never should be any at a Thanksgiving dinner. Neither did any fish follow where no soup led the way. You began with your chicken pie and your roast turkey. You ate as much as you could, and you then ate what you could of mince pie, squash pie, Marlborough pie, cranberry tart, and plum pudding. Then you went to work on the fruits as you could. Here, in parenthesis, I will say to young Americans that the use of dried fruits at the table was much more frequent in those days than in these. Dates, prunes, raisins, figs, and nuts held a much more prominent place in a handsome dessert than they do now. Recollect that oranges were all brought from the West Indies or from the Mediterranean in sailing vessels, and were by no means served in the profusion with which they are served now. It has not much to do with a Thanksgiving dinner, but bananas as I have said above, somewhere, were wholly unknown.

With such devices the children at the side-table and the elders at the large table whiled away the time till it was quite dark, and it might well be that the lamps were lighted. Observe, gas was wholly unknown in private residences. And when at last the last philopoena had been given between two of the children, or the last "roast turkey" had been broken out of an English walnut and saved as a curiosity, all parties slid from their chairs, or rose up from them, as the length of their legs might be, and adjourned to the large parlor again.

At the bottom of my heart I think that here came a period in which the elders quailed. I think it was rather hard for them to maintain the conversation about genealogy and lost inheritances. But we children never quailed. We either returned to the picture-books or we sat in the corner and told stories, or possibly the expert cousins, who were skilled in the fine arts, drew pictures for us. I have not the slightest recollection, either at that first Thanksgiving or on any subsequent Thanksgiving of childhood, of any moment of tediousness or gloom, such as I have since found to hang over even the bravest in the midst of a high festivity. Before long we would be in the corner playing commerce, or old maid, or possibly "slap everlasting"; or the Game of Human Life would be produced, with the teetotum, and one would find himself in the stocks, or in a gambling-room, or in prison perhaps, or happily, at the age of sixty-three years, in glory. Memorandum: It is seven years since I passed that grand climacteric of

7 x 9 with which the teetotum games ended,
and I am not in glory yet, unless the beauty
of an October day, when leaves of gold shine
out between me and the blue heavens may be
considered glory enough for one who believes
that this world was made by a good God.
There was nothing to prevent blind-man's-buff,
but that the elders had to have their share of
the room.   In later days charades came in,
and it is now forty years since I have assisted
at a Thanksgiving, without annually acting the
part of *Young Lochinvar*, or *Lord Ullin*, or of
the "Captain bold of Halifax."   But this I
did not do when I was four years old.   Of
those first Thanksgiving Days my memories
are simply of undisguised delight.   I wonder
now that I did not die the day after the first
of them from having eaten five times as much
as I should have done.   But there seems to be
a good Providence which watches over boys
and girls, as over idiots and drunken people.
This is sure, that I have survived to tell the
story.

Social existence in all forms of civilization

requires a certain knowledge of dancing; and in conventional civilization this dancing is not left to the spontaneous joy of children, but, willingly or unwillingly, they have to be taught to dance. This fell upon us as upon other children, and to the very end of his life Mr. Lorenzo Papanti, cordial, graceful, and dignified old man, remembered kindly that I was one of the first four pupils whom he had in Boston. He has become so far an historical character to many of the best in Boston that the reader will excuse me if I give a few words to his dancing-school. It was in Montgomery Place, now Bosworth Street; I think in the very house which was removed to open the passage through to what we called Cooke's Court, and what the present generation calls Chapman Place. It was in the third story of that house, where a partition had been cut away to make a hall large enough for a dancing-school. The papering at one end still differed from the papering at the other. To this hall of Terpsichore I repaired with three others, and we were the only pupils on the first Thursday afternoon of our attendance. On the next

Saturday there arrived more, one of them one of my brothers in baptism, of whom I have already spoken ; and from that time the school increased, and, as one is glad to say, maintains at this moment, under the direction of another generation, the high and well-deserved regard and esteem of everybody in Boston who knows anything about it. This hall was near our house, so that we could always go on foot. But there was a rather tragic story in the family of the school of M. Labassé, to which my older brother and sister went, which was so far away that they had to be sent in a carriage. Unfortunately in the jolting of the carriage they were shaken off the seats, and they were so small that they could not climb up on them again before they arrived at their destination. Thus early was the art of graceful movement impressed upon them.

For me, dancing-school shared in the dislike with which I regarded all other schools. Dear Mrs. Papanti—I remember her with gratitude to this moment—did her best for me, but never was a pupil less likely to add to the reputation of an institution. The school was afterwards removed to Bulfinch Place, where the Papantis had an elegant house. I was at that time bribed to attend by being told I might take a book with me to read. One afternoon, when the boys were carrying on awfully, dear Mrs. Papanti bore down upon us, and said, "Why is it that Master Hale is so quiet, while Master Champernoon behaves so badly?" and looked over my shoulder, to see that I was reading "Guy Mannering." "Ah!" she cried, "I will give Master Champernoon a set of the Waverley novels if he will behave as well as Master Hale does!" But alas, Master Champernoon was one of the boys who enjoyed dancing, and wanted to dance, and had unwarranted arrangements with the girls with regard to partners, and so on, while Master Hale detested the whole thing. Good soul, she did her best in dragging me about, as a favorite pupil, in the waltz; but my poor head swam, and I think my partners, from that day to this, have generally preferred to "stand through a waltz," when they have found the alternative was sharing it with me.

All this led, of course, to little evening par-

ties of the boys and girls, just as it does now.
The boys would stand at the foot of the stairs
and in the entries, just as they do now, and
maiden aunts would make incursions upon
them to tell them that they must take partners, just as they do now. They took these
partners, and then retired from the field to
similar clusters, to be broken up again, just as
they do now.

I have tried to describe in my story "East
and West" the way in which refreshments were
generally served at evening parties, unless
these were on the grandest scale. There
would frequently be such a party without
a proper supper-table. I believe this was
largely due to the fact that, in very few houses
in Boston then, was there a special dining-room.
People dined in their back parlors, and when
the house was given up to dancing the back
parlor was not available as a supper-room. At
the simpler parties to which boys and girls
went, in place of the supper a little procession of servants brought in large trays with
cake of different kinds, even with ice cream,
perhaps with jelly or blanc mange, with wine

or lemonade ; and these processions recurred half a dozen times in the course of the evening.

Another function which brought young people together, and brought them together with older people, was the arrangement for evening lectures. These were much more familiar and homelike than the lectures of to-day, to which we go hardly with any idea of social enjoyment. But, as I have intimated, the "march of intellect" had begun. One feature of the march of intellect was the introduction of lectures for people who wanted to learn something. They were exactly what is called the university extension system to-day, which I observe, however, is spoken of everywhere as if it were an entirely new invention. A lecture course is now undertaken by a director, or *entrepreneur*, who means to provide entertainment for the people. He does not pretend to teach the people ; he proposes to entertain them. Therefore, if his course consists of eight lectures, he provides eight different entertaining speakers ; and this makes almost a class of men, each of whom has a few entertaining addresses prepared with this definite purpose. But in the earlier days of what we called the lecture system, or the lyceum, a body of public-spirited men, who really wanted to improve the education of the community, banded themselves together into a society for that purpose. This society, among other instrumentalities, established courses of lectures, generally in the winter, for the instruction of the people.

In Boston such lectures had been heralded by courses arranged by individuals. Dr. Jacob Bigelow had courses on botany ; Henry Ware gave a course of very popular lectures on Palestine ; Edward Everett delivered lectures on Greek antiquities ; and there were other similar courses, just as there might be now, if anybody would attend them. The success of these courses showed that a systematic arrangement might be made for courses of popular lectures in the evenings, and such were, in fact, carried on by different societies for a period of years. They culminated in the great success which Mr. John Lowell achieved, in the establishment of the Lowell Institute ;

and I suppose it was this foundation which broke down at once all weaker foundations with the same purpose. It does its work so well that nobody in Boston need have any tears for them. I remember the Society for the Promotion of Useful Knowledge, the Mercantile Library Association, the Mechanics' Apprentices' Association, the Natural History Society, and the Historical Society, as maintaining such courses of lectures as I describe. There would be from ten to fifteen lectures in a course. The tickets for the cheapest were fifty cents a course ; for the others they were a dollar, or even two dollars. At our house this made no difference, because tickets to everything—concerts, lectures, and the rest— were sent to the newspaper office, and practically we children went to any such entertainments as we liked.

One of these societies would arrange a course of lectures. The whole course might be on chemistry. I remember such a course from Professor Webster. It was conducted with all his brilliant power of experiment, and listened to with enthusiasm by four or five

hundred people.   I remember another course
by John Farrar on the steam-engine.   I heard
in the Useful Knowledge course several of
Mr. Waldo Emerson's biographical lectures.
The Useful Knowledge course would be perhaps on Tuesday evening, the Mercantile
Library on Wednesday, the Mechanics' on
Thursday.   Eventually halls were built specially for such lectures.   There was one favorite hall in the Masonic Temple, which is now
occupied, as rebuilt, by Messrs. Stearns.   I
suppose this hall would hold five hundred
people.   The seats rose rapidly, as in the
lecture-room of a medical college, so that
people could see all the experiments or pictures on the platform.

To such an entertainment you went, and if
you were old enough you took a friend of the
other sex.   You arrived there half an hour
before the lecture began, and walked from
seat to seat, talking with the people whom you
found there.   After the lecture had gone on
half an hour or more there was a recess, and
again you walked about from seat to seat,
perhaps chose another seat, if the first had not

been satisfactory. At the end of a lecture of maybe an hour and a half in length you went home with anybody who chose to invite you. At the house you went to there was the invariable dish of oysters, or crackers and cheese, or whatever was the evening meal of that particular evening. And thus the lyceum lecture of that time played a quite important part in the social arrangements of growing boys and girls.

Of its advantage as a system of instruction I can say hardly too much. Of course the instruction given was superficial. I have lived seventy years in the world, and I have never found any instruction that was not superficial. But it was instruction ; it was instruction given by first-rate men, who knew how to teach ; and it was systematic instruction. The lecturer of to-day takes an epigrammatic phrase for his subject, as he calls it ; it is the "Philosophy of Mathematics," or it is the "Mathematics of Philosophy." He speaks well, he brings in interesting stories, he gives a little information, and the public which sees him and hears

him is amused.   Someone asked James Rus-
sell Lowell once whether he supposed that
the average audience of an interior town in
New York cared much for Beaumont and
Fletcher.   He said very frankly : " I do not
suppose they care for Beaumont and Fletcher
at all.   But I suppose they have heard of me
and want to see me, and a good way to see me
is to pay for my lecture, sit in front of me,
and see and hear me for the hour in which I
am reading something which interests me."
This is very genuine ; it is all right ; it is a
good bit of public entertainment for people
who have been tired to death by the work
of the day.   But it is not instruction.   Dear
Starr King used to say : " A lyceum lecture
consists of five parts of sense and five of nonsense.   There are not more than five people in
New England who know how to mix them.
But I am one of the five."   All lecturers do
not keep to his recipe.

On the other hand, I believe that if we could
wipe out the whole nonsense of the evening
lessons from the school curriculum ; if we
could make teachers teach, where now they

simply hear the lesson which somebody else
has taught; if then we would reserve our
evenings for instructing intelligent boys and
girls in the fundamental principles of a good
many things which are best taught by lectures,
I believe that we should improve the system
of public instruction to-day. It would require
a good deal of work on the part of a great
many intelligent people. Possibly some time
there will be a school committee which will
think such an enterprise worthy of attention.

A few years ago I looked in, late in the
evening, upon a pretty little party of one of
the largest classes in my own Sunday-school.
I met there perhaps thirty of the sweetest and
most charming of the younger women in Boston. They had assembled at the invitation of
their teacher, who had recently travelled in the
East, and they had been spending the evening
in conversation with one another and with
her, and in examining the curiosities, and
especially the photographs, which she had
brought from Egypt, Syria, and Greece. In
this large and brilliant company I was the
only gentleman. At half-past ten, after a

little supper, we all gathered to go home.
Comparing the detail of Boston life with what
it would have been fifty years before, I was
interested to see that these young ladies all
went home without escort from the other sex.
Some of them had ordered their carriages ;
many took street cars, which passed the house
in one direction or the other, and which would
leave them within a block of their own residences.   It is certainly highly creditable to
Boston that a body of women, young or old,
can use the evening in such a way, and can
disperse to their homes at such an hour with
no companionship but what they give to one
another, and with no hazard of insult.

But I thought then, and I have often said
since, that such a social order was wholly
unlike the social order in which I grew up.
When I was a boy of eight, or nine, or ten, no
sister of mine would have gone to take tea
with a friend but one of her brothers would
have been detailed to go for her and bring her
home at eight or nine o'clock.   I am quite
clear that in those days the life of young
people involved a great deal more of the visit-

ing of both sexes together than it does now. I do not mean to speak of the life of boys of fifteen years old and over. I speak of the life of boys of all ages, from five or six years upward.

The function of tea-parties was quite different from that of dinner-parties. You would invite two or three boys and girls who were friends of your children to come and take tea, where now you would hardly invite children of the same age to come and dine. Now if this function happened to be exercised in the house of old-fashioned people it had some rather queer attendants—or what would seem queer to the boy of the present day. For instance, one of the relics of Revolutionary times was the general impression that no boy could ever serve his country, unless he were trained as a public speaker. I think this is true now, and it was known to be true then. Consequently when you were at such a party as I have described, the evening's entertainment of playing old maid, teetotum games, jack-straws, or whatever might occupy the young people, would be interrupted, from time to time, by an appeal to the boys of the

"MASTER EDWARD, THE COMPANY WOULD LIKE TO HEAR YOU SPEAK A PIECE."—*Page* 161.

party to "speak a piece" for the benefit of
the elders. There was a certain compliment
implied in being asked to "speak a piece,"
but it was not a great compliment, for every
boy was asked, not to say compelled, to do so.
It would have been bad form to decline to
speak, quite as much as it would be to sit at a
dinner-table and decline to eat anything before
you, as if it were of a quality poorer than that
to which you were accustomed.

Accordingly you had one or two "pieces"
in mind which you were prepared to "speak."
When you were called upon—when the old
ladies, at their side of the room, had made up
their minds that it was time for this exercise
to go forward—you were told, "Master Edward" (or Master Oliver, or Master Alexander), "the company would like to have you
speak a piece." You demurred as little as
you could, you went into a corner, you made
a bow, and you spoke a piece. You then went
back to your cards or other entertainment. I
do not remember that the girls sang songs, as
it seems to me they should have done, under
the circumstances.

At such a little party, again, invariably the
tray was brought in as the evening went by,
and you ate the nuts and raisins or figs, which
were generally something you did not have at
home. Perhaps this is always one of the
charms of social life.

There may be, by the way, no other opportunity in these papers to quote the amusing
passage from Dr. Palfrey on salt codfish. It
is in his admirable chapter on New England
life, in which he followed the example of
Macaulay's celebrated chapter describing the
family institutions of England.

Forty years ago I was so situated as to know un-
commonly well the habits of different classes of people
in different parts of the country. Till a later period
than this the most ceremonious Boston feast was never
set out on Saturday (then the common dinner-party day)
without the dunfish at one end of the table; abundance,
variety, pomp of other things, but that unfailingly. It
was a sort of New England point of honor; and luxuri-
ous livers pleased themselves, over their nuts and wine,
with the thought that, while suiting their palates, they
had been doing their part in a wide combination to
maintain the fisheries and create a naval strength.

There was one function of those days which
has been admirably improved in the customs

of later days.   Franklin left a small fund to
the city, to be expended in medals for the most
deserving scholars.   The Franklin medal was
first awarded in 1792, is awarded to the present
time, and is a good badge of honor to the
genuine Boston boy.   The school committee
and the government of the city dined together,
on the day of the school anniversary, in Faneuil Hall, and the boys who received the
Franklin medals were then first initiated into
the forms of a public dinner.   There must
have been some sort of a procession—I do not
know, for I never had a Franklin medal—and
the boys sat in Faneuil Hall and heard the
speaking.   But as years went on, after the
time of which I speak, and particularly after
the girls began to receive city medals, it was
seen that a much pleasanter entertainment
could be devised for the children than a feast
at which the officers of the city government
took the principal part, and in which almost
all parties drank more wine than was good
for them.   And in these later days the mayor
holds a great reception in the large Mechanics' Hall; he gives to every graduating

girl a bouquet, and the boys and girls dance together to music which the city provides. I mention the contrast, because I am quite sure that in the years between 1826 and 1837 there would have been a religious prejudice in some quarters against dancing, which would have prevented any such public celebration.

The boys were in touch with the large public in their unauthorized and unrecognized connection with the fire department. Boston was still a wooden town, and the danger of fire was, as it is in all American cities, constantly present. There hung in our front entry two leather buckets ; in each of them was certain apparatus which a person might need if he were in a burning house. Strange to say, there was a bed-key, that he might take down a bedstead if it were necessary. These were relics of a time when my father had been a member of one of the private fire companies. In those associations each man was bound to attend at any fire where the property of other members of the association was in danger ; and there were traditions of father's having been present at the great Court Street fire, for instance.

But these fire clubs either died out or became social institutions, as the Fire Club in
Worcester exists to this day; and nothing was
left but the bucket as a sort of memorial
of a former existence.

Before our day the volunteer fire department system of Boston had been created, and
there were similar systems in all large cities.
Of course we boys supposed that ours was the
best in the world ; each boy in Boston supposed that the engine nearest his house was
the best engine in the world, and that, on
occasion, it could throw water higher than
any other engine. It could likewise, on
occasion, pump dry any engine that was in
line with it. I need not say that these notions
of the boys were simply superstitions, wholly
unfounded in fact. Our engine was the *New
York*. The engine-house was one of a curious
mass of public buildings that occupied the
place where Franklin's statue now stands, in
front of what was the court-house of that day.
There was no electric fire alarm in those early
days. The moment a fire broke out everybody who had any lungs ran up the street or

down the street, or both ways, crying "Fire !"
and as soon as the churches could be opened,
all the bells in Boston began to ring.   Then
the company which was to drag the *New York*
to the fire began to assemble at its house, and
naturally there was great pride in seeing that
your engine was first in place.   You learned
where the fire was, not by any signal, but by the
rumor of the street.   It was at the North End,
or at the South End, or on the wharves, or on
" Nigger Hill."   As soon as boys and men, of
whatever connection, arrived, sufficient to drag
the engine, it started, under the direction of
such officer of the company as might be present.   The members of the company had no
uniforms, so far as I remember ; they joined
the lines as quickly as they could, but there
were always enough people to pull.   As I have
intimated, it was everybody's business to
attend at the fire.

When you arrived at the spot there would
be a general caucus as to the method of attack,
yet I think there were people in command.
Afterwards a gentleman named Amory, highly
respected by all of us, was chief engineer.

Whatever the caucus directed was done, with as much efficiency as was possible under such democratic institutions. But, in the first place, the probability was that there was no water near. The Jamaica Pond aqueduct carried water in log pipes to the lower levels of the city ; but, for fully half the city, there was no such supply, and wells had to be relied upon. Every engine, therefore, which was good for anything was a "suction engine," as it was called; that is, it was able to pump from a well, as well as able to throw water to an indefinite height. The engine that arrived first repaired to the well best known in that neighborhood, or, if the occasion were fortunate, to the sea, and began to pump. The engine that arrived next took station next to this, and pumped from it through a long line of hose ; and so successive engines carried the water to the place where some foreman directed it upon the flames. It was thus that the different engines attained their celebrity, as one pumped the tub of another dry, while the unfortunate members were "working the brakes" to their best to keep it full.

The buckets of which I have spoken were
the remains of a yet earlier period, when
people formed themselves in line to the well
or to the sea, and passed buckets backward
and forward—full if they were going toward
the fire, empty if they were going away ; and
the water was thus thrown upon such flames
as chose to wait for it.

When one writes this, one wonders that
Boston was not burned down four times a
year ; indeed, there were many bad fires in
those days. The system called out some of
the most energetic and public-spirited young
fellows of the town, and after a while they
were exempt from service in the militia. Well
they might be, for their service as firemen was
far more valuable to the community, and far
more oppressive in time and health, than any
service in the militia of those days. They felt
their power, and asserted it once too often.
In the mayoralty of Mr. Samuel A. Eliot a
company did something it should not have
done, or refused to do something it was told
to do ; with a firm hand, he turned them
all out, and created the system of the fire

department of to-day, in which every man is
paid for his services, and may be regularly
called upon, whether he will or no, as a ser-
vant of the city. The introduction of steam
fire-engines, and a sufficient supply of water,
would in themselves have been enough to
revolutionize the whole of the primitive
method of extinguishing fire, had no such
revolt of the fire companies compelled a revolution.

I need hardly say that the old method
interested to the full every boy in town. If
his father and mother would let him, he
attended the fire, where he could at least scream
"Fire!" if he could not do anything else. If
a boy were big enough he was permitted
almost to kill himself by working at the brakes.
This was the most exhausting method for the
application of human power that has been
contrived; but there was power enough to be
wasted, and, until the introduction of steam,
it was everywhere used. It is still used on
board ships which have no steam power.
Every enterprising boy regarded it as the one
wish of his life that he might be eighteen years

old, so that he could join the company in his particular neighborhood ; and even if he had not attained that age, he attached himself to the company as a sort of volunteer aid, and, as I say, was permitted, as a favor, to assist in running through the streets, dragging at the long rope which drew the engine.

CHAPTER VII.

THE WORLD NEAR BOSTON.

THE Broad Street Riot, so called, on the afternoon of June 11, 1837, was an event which of course had great interest for the boys of the period. It was the fortune of very few of them, however, who were decently brought up, to have any hand in that conflict; for, as I have said in another chapter of these recollections, people in those days went to "meeting" as regularly in the afternoon as they did in the morning.

If there should be need to-day for the sudden appearance of the military forces of Boston on a Sunday afternoon I think that the officers of those forces would be looked for quite as readily at the Browning Club or a chess club, or possibly even exercising their horses somewhere within ten miles of Boston, as at any place of public worship. But my whole personal recollection of the Broad

Street Riot is that, of a sudden, the bell of
Brattle Street Church struck "backward,"
and the gentlemen who were of the First Regiment rose and left their seats, and went down
to the armory at Faneuil Hall to join their
companies, not to say lead them. It was said,
and I believe truly, that a sergeant formed the
first men who arrived in skeletons of companies, and in a skeleton of a regiment. George
Tyler Bigelow, afterwards chief justice of the
Supreme Court, was the first commissioned
officer who arrived. He was a lieutenant in
the New England Guards or the Light Infantry. He ordered the regiment out of the
armory, and commanded it till he met a superior officer. The story was that the command
changed half a dozen times before the regiment reached Broad Street, where firemen and
Irishmen were fighting. Of which I saw and
remember nothing. But the departure of
those gentlemen from church, whom we would
have joined so gladly, fixed the whole affair in
our memories. In a boy journal of the time,
I find the comment, after I had read the newspaper account, " The Irish got well beaten, but

the firemen appear to have been as much in
the wrong as they."

In all these reminiscences I am well aware
that our lives were much less affected by the
daily news from abroad than are the lives of
people now.   Certainly Boston regarded itself
more as a metropolis than it does now.   And
for this there was good reason : for Boston had
much less connection with the rest of the
world than it has now.   It had a foreign commerce, and the average boy expected to go to
sea some time or other.   But I recollect times
when a vessel from England brought thirty-
five days' news ; all through the time of which
I am writing it took three days for a letter to
go to Washington ; and although people no
longer offered prayers for their friends when
they were going to New York, still a journey
to New York was comparatively a rare business.   In my third year in college I wanted
to send a parcel of dried plants to a botanist
in New York.   There was no proper "express,"
and I asked it as a personal favor of a young
man named Harnden, whom I knew as a conductor on the Boston and Worcester Railroad,

that he would give the parcel to someone who would give it to someone else who would give it to my correspondent. It was because Mr. Harnden had so many such personal favors in hand that he established Harnden's Express, which was, I think, the first of the organized expresses which existed in this country.

I find it difficult to make the Boston boy or girl of to-day understand how different was Boston life, thus shut in from the rest of the world, from our life, when, as I suppose, at least one hundred thousand people enter Boston every day, and as many leave it for some place outside.

As late as May, 1845, when I was twenty-three years old, I had an engagement to go from Boston to Worcester Saturday afternoon. I was to preach there the next day. When, at three o'clock, I came to the station of the Worcester road, there was an announcement that, from some accident on the line above, no train would leave until Monday. The three o'clock train, observe, was the latest train of Saturday. I crossed Boston to the Fitchburg station and took the train for

Groton or Littleton.   There I took a stage for
Lancaster, where I slept.*   In the morning,
with a Worcester man who had been caught in
Boston as I was, I took a wagon early, and we
two drove across to Worcester.   That is to
say, as late as 1845 there were but two men in
Boston to whom it was necessary that they
should go to Worcester that afternoon.   And
this was ten years after railroad communication had been established.

Before railroad communication was open,
intercourse with other States, or with what
now seem neighboring cities, was very infrequent.   In 1832 my father went to Schenectady
to see the Albany and Schenectady Railroad,
and, I believe, to order some cars for the Boston and Worcester road.   He also went to
New York City on the business of that road.

* As I write these memoranda, in September, 1892, just as
we have heard of Mr. Whittier's death, there is a certain
interest in saying that it was on this occasion that I first met
him.   As the handful of passengers entered the stage which
was to take us to Lancaster, Mr. Whittier was one of the number.   He did not tell his name to anyone, and it was many
years before I knew that he was one of those whose pleasant
conversation enlivened the dark ride.   I can hardly say that I
saw him, but he was kind enough afterwards always to remember that I made his acquaintance on that occasion. .

I think he had been to that city but once since 1805, when he went there on his way from Northampton to Troy. Yet if anybody was to travel he would have been apt to. He was a journalist, intensely interested in internal improvement. He had a large business correspondence in New York, and was well known there. I was myself nineteen years old when I first visited New York.

In 1841 I had a chance to overhaul the old register at the hotel at Stafford Springs in Connecticut. Stafford Springs was, and is, a watering-place of a modest sort, where is a good, strong iron spring—good for boys with warts, and indeed for anyone who needs iron in his blood. It was quite the fashion to go to Stafford Springs from different parts of New England, in the earlier part of the century. In this old register it was interesting to see how universal was the custom by which people came there in their own carriages. What followed was that people who had no carriages of their own hardly travelled for pleasure at all.

So was it that, in the years of my boyhood, Boston people, with very few exceptions, lived

in Boston the year round. People did not
care to go to the theatre in midsummer, and I
think the theatres were generally closed for
six or eight weeks when the days were
longest. Perhaps Boston used the matchless
advantages of her bay more when she had
little communication with points beyond it.
Perhaps the entertainments of the bay seemed
more important because there were few, if any,
excursions for pleasure excepting those which
the water offered.

Nahant was seized upon as a sea-shore resort
as early as 1819. The sea serpent had appeared
in 1817. The hotel on the south-eastern point,
long since burned down, was a pretty, piazza-
guarded building ; and, as the steamboat
Housatonic went down to Nahant every morning, and came back every night, a day at
Nahant made a charming summer expedition, which we young folks relied upon at
least once a year. At Nahant, at Chelsea
Beach, at Nantasket, at Sandwich, and at
Gloucester I made my acquaintance with the
real ocean. At Nahant I made my first
acquaintance with the joy of the bowling

alley, and first saw the game of billiards.
By the way, I remember that, in lecturing to
my class in college, as late as 1837, Professor
Lovering had to tell the class, as a fact which
half of them did not know, that when one
billiard-ball strikes another it may stop itself,
while it communicates its motion to the other.
I doubt if half the young men who heard him
had ever seen a billiard-table at that time.

There were but one or two steamboats in the
harbor, so that the "excursion" of to-day was
very infrequent.   But all the more would people go down the bay for fishing-parties, on
sailing vessels—more, I should think, than
they do now.   Perhaps there was something
in foreign commerce which gave to those
engaged in it a sort of absolute freedom sometimes, sandwiched in with hard work at others,
in an alternate remission of work and play,
which the modern merchant seldom enjoys.
Your ship came in from Liverpool or from
Calcutta, and you and all your staff, down to
the boy who swept out the office and trimmed
the lamps, were busy, morning, noon, and
night, till her cargo was disposed of, and per-

haps till she was fitted for another voyage. But then, if no other of your ships arrived, there would be a lull; and if Tom, Dick, or Harry came in to propose a fishing-party you were ready.

However this may be, the history and experiences of such parties made a considerable element of summer life. The anecdote of General Moreau belongs to them, and I will print it, though it was told a generation before my time. When General Moreau was in exile from France he came on his travels to Boston. Among other entertainments he was taken down the bay on a fishing-party. As they dined, or after dinner, excellent Colonel Messenger, whose singing is still remembered with pleasure, was asked to favor the company with a song, and he sang the fine old English song of "To-morrow." The refrain is in the words :

> To-morrow, to-morrow,
> Will be everlasting to-morrow.

The French exile did not understand English as well as he did the art of war, and when

Colonel Messenger came to these words, at
the end of each verse, he supposed, naturally
enough, that he was hearing a song made in
his own honor :

> To Moreau, to Moreau,
> Je n'entends pas bien, mais to Moreau.

And so he rose, as each verse closed, put his
hand to his heart, blushed, and bowed grate-
fully, as to a personal compliment. And his
hosts were too courteous to undeceive him.

The Harvard Navy Club, an institution long
since dead, used to "go down," as the abbre-
viated phrase was, every year. "Go down"
was short for "go down the bay and fish."
The Navy Club was a club of those men who
received no college honors. The laziest man in
a class was the "Lord High Admiral"; the
next to the laziest was the "Admiral of the
Blue," and so on.

Perhaps there are not so many fish in the
bay as there were then. Perhaps I am not so
much interested in the boys who take them.
But I do not see, when I cross the bridge to
East Cambridge, any boy patiently sitting on

the rail waiting to catch flounders, as I have done many a happy afternoon. Perhaps, as civilization has come in, the flounders have stayed lower down the bay.

Travelling, in short, was done by retail in those days, and such combinations as those of to-day, by which a hundred thousand people are thrown upon Boston daily, and as many taken away, were wholly unknown, not to say not dreamed of. Retail travelling, if we are to use that expression, had some points of interest which do not enliven the career of a traveller who is boxed up in a train with three hundred and ninety-nine others, all of them to be delivered, "right side up with care," at the place they wish to go to, while none of them have what John Locke would call an "adequate idea" of the places on the way, if indeed any of them have any idea.

The first of such expeditions which I remember, excepting one on the Middlesex Canal, which has been referred to, was in August and September of 1826, when my father took all of us—that is, my mother and four children—to Sandwich, where he was going to enjoy a

week's shooting. The other gentlemen of the
party were Daniel Webster, Judge Story, and
Judge Fay. Mr. Webster took his family
with him ; I think the other gentlemen did
not take theirs. All of us stayed at Fessen-
den's tavern—charmingly comfortable then, I
fancy, as I know it was afterwards. My early
memories of the expedition are quite distinct.
It was here and then that I first fired the gun
which is the oldest sporting gun here at Matu-
nuck ; and a good gun it is, if people are not
above an old-fashioned percussion cap. But
in those days it had a flintlock. The general
use of what are now unknown to young sports-
men, percussion caps, belongs some years
later. The bigger boys, Fletcher Webster and
my brother Nathan, would be taken out with
the gentlemen to hold the horses (in *chaises*,
observe) on the beach, while their fathers
walked about and shot what they might.
But we little fellows stayed at home, to be
lifted to the seventh heaven if a loaded gun
were brought home at night which we might
aim and fire at a shingle. For us and the
girls the principal occupation, I remember,

was playing dinner and tea with the pretty glassware which the Sandwich works were just beginning to make. I believe I have somewhere at this day some specimens of their work for children.

On this expedition we went and returned, some in the "stage" and some in my father's chaise—making the journey, I think, in a day. But generally, with so large a host as ours— which included Fullum—we went on the summer journey, whatever it was, in what was then, as it is indeed now, called a "barouche." The names "landau," "victoria," and the like were, I think, unknown. As this business was by no means peculiar to our family, and as it belongs to a civilization quite unlike ours, I will describe it in detail.

We were to go to Cape Ann, and for perhaps a week to take such comfort as the great "tavern" at Gloucester would give. Observe that the word "tavern" was still used, as I think it now is where a tavern exists in the heart of New England, for what the Englishman calls an "inn." We talk now of the Wayside Inn, the Wayland Inn, and so on,

but this is all in a labored, artificial, and indeed
foreign speech introduced from England within
a generation past.   To prepare for such an
expedition Fullum would be sent from stable
to stable to hire the best barouche he could
find, and a span of horses. Happy the boy
who selected himself, or was selected by des-
tiny, to accompany him on this tour of inspection !   When the happy morning arrived
Fullum brought round his carriage and horses
early, fastened on the trunk behind—for
I think there never was but one ; and the
two elders, and in this case of Cape Ann
the five children, with books and hand bag-
gage, always with maps of the country,
were packed away in and on the carriage.
Both of us boys, of course, sat on the box
with Fullum, who drove.   If, on any such
occasion, there were a very little boy, Fullum
would arrange a duplicate set of reins for the
special use of the youngster, which were
attached, not to the horses' bits, but to the
rings on the pads. In this particular expedition to Cape Ann we stopped at the Lynn
Mineral Spring Hotel, long since abandoned,

I think, and reached Gloucester only perhaps on the second day.

What happened to the old people there I am sure I do not know. To us children there were those ineffable delights of playing with the ocean, the kindest, safest, and best playmate which any child can have. Sandwich had given us only the first taste of it. Here we had our first real knowledge of what sea-urchins are, and what people call "sand dollars," horseshoe crabs, cockles, rays' eggs, and the various sea-weeds, from devil's aprons up or down. The cape had not assumed the grandeur of a summer watering-place. The modern names were unknown. There was no Rockport or Pigeon Cove to go to. It was Sandy Bay or Squam to which one drove. I remember the ejaculation of some fishermen's children, as they saw the barouche for the first time : "What is it? It aint the mail, and it aint a shay."

At that time, and certainly as late as 1842, a group of children in the country, if they saw a carriage approaching, would arrange themselves hastily in a line on one side of the road and "make their manners." That is, they would all bow as the carriage passed. The last time that I remember seeing this was in 1842, in Hampshire County, as the stage passed by. It was done good-naturedly, with no sign of deference, but rather, I should say, as a pleasant recognition of human brotherhood in a lonely region—as two men, if they were not Englishmen, might bow to each other, wherever they were far from other men.

In our particular family an annual journey was made to my grandfather's house in Westhampton, a pleasant town among the hills in Hampshire County, where my father was born. He took his wife there in his chaise when they were married, in 1816, and hardly a summer passed, until 1837, when he did not make the same journey with his whole family. This then numbered seven children, besides himself and my mother, and of course Fullum. To my father it was a matter of pride that on the last of these journeys we went on his own railroad to Worcester. In 1835 the carriage was taken on a truck on the passenger train, in which we rode; but I need not say that Fullum

"CHILDREN IN THE COUNTRY WOULD ARRANGE THEMSELVES HASTILY
AND MAKE THEIR MANNERS."—*Page 186.*

preferred to sit in the carriage all the way, and
did so.

There was a charm in such half-vagrant
journeying about which the Raymond tourist
knows nothing.   There was no sending in
advance for rooms, and you took your chances
at the tavern, where you arrived, perhaps, at
nine o'clock at night.   It may be imagined
that the sudden appearance at the country
tavern of a party of ten, of all ages from three
months upwards, was an event of interest.   In
those times the selectmen knew what they
meant, when they said that no person should
dispense liquor who did not provide for travellers.   Practically it was a convenience to any
village to have a place where travellers could
stay ; and practically the people of that village said to the man whom they licensed to
sell liquor, "If you have this privilege, you
must provide a decent place of entertainment
for strangers."   One man kept the tavern,
perhaps, for his life long.   It had its reputation as good or poor, and you avoided certain
towns because So-and-So did not keep a good
house.   The practical difficulty of such travel-

ling in New England now, is that you are by
no means sure of finding a comfortable place
to sleep when your day's journey is over.
The New England tavern of the old fashion
held its own to the most advantage in later
times in the State of Maine, on the roads back
into the lumber region, and I dare say such
comfortable houses for travellers may be found
there now.

These country taverns always had signs,
generally swinging from a post with a cross-
bar, in front of the house. The sign might be
merely the name of the keeper; this was a sad
disappointment to young travellers. More
probably it was the picture of the American
eagle or of a rising sun. Neptune rising from
the sea was a favorite device. I remember at
Worcester the Elephant. The portrait of General Wolfe still hangs at the Newburyport
tavern, and there remain some General Wash-
ingtons. After I was a man I had occasion to
travel a good deal one summer in Northern
Vermont, where the tavern signs still existed.
Almost without exception their devices were
of the American eagle with his wings spread,

or of the American eagle holding the English
lion in chains, or of the lion chained without
any American eagle. These were in memory
of Macomb's and McDonough's victories at
Plattsburg and on the lake. They also, perhaps, referred to the fact that most of these
taverns were supported by the wagons of
smugglers, who, in their good, large peddlers'
carts, provided themselves with English goods
in Canada, which they sold on our side of the
line. In our generation one is more apt to see
a tavern sign in a museum than hanging on a
gallows-tree.

Meandering along through Leicester, Spen-
cer, Belchertown, Ware, Amherst, Northampton, or some of these places, we arrived
at my grandfather's pretty home in Westhampton on the morning of the third day.
Then, for three or four days, came absolute
and infinite joy. We had cousins there just
our own ages of whom we were very fond.
For the time of our visit they gave themselves,
without stint or hindrance, to the entertainment of their friends from Boston. First of
all, horses were to be provided, and saddles,

that we boys might ride. Little did the
country boys understand what joy it was to us
to find ourselves scampering over the hills.
Then there was the making of traps for wood-
chucks. If it chose to rain we were in the
great workshop of the farm, using such tools
as we had never seen at home. In the evening
there were "hunt the slipper" and "blind-
man's-buff," the latter an entertainment which
we could follow even on Sunday evening, as I
believe I have said, and follow then with more
enthusiasm than on other evenings, because
other cousins and the children of neighbors
came in to join with us. In that New England
parsonage—never so called, by the way—the
old Connecticut customs prevailed, and "the
Sabbath" began promptly as the sun went
down on Saturday night, and was well ended
when the sun set on Sunday. The hills of
Westhampton are high, and sunset on Sunday
evening came early.

So it was that the great joy of life was the
visit at grandfather's every summer. My
grandfather was the minister of this town for
fifty-seven years. I think I saw the dear old

gentleman last in 1834. It must have been
in 1837, after his death, that we made the last
visit there, when my grandmother was still
living. I did not myself return to Westhampton for fifty years, when it was to preach
in his pulpit. It was pleasant to find that,
after two generations, the people of the town
remembered him fondly. I found the pulpit
of the meeting-house and the chancel behind
it decorated with flowers, and the word "Welcome," wrought in flowers, hung above me.
So I went back to the happiest days of my
New England boyhood.

I have already alluded to the infrequency of
communication between this country home—for
it was such to all of us children—and the home
in Boston. The cousins in the country, when
autumn came, would not forget us in Boston,
and would crack butternuts and walnuts for
us, of kinds they thought we should not have,
pick out the great meats, and pack them carefully to be sent down. Such a box would be
sent to Northampton, and put on board a
boat which went to Hartford. There it would
be put on board a sloop, in which it was to sail

out of the Connecticut River and around Cape
Cod to Boston.   In the same sloop was perhaps
a keg of my grandmother's apple sauce, or
some other treasure from the farm.   Great joy
for us if all these pleasant memorials arrived
in time ; great sorrow if a letter came, stating
that the sloop was frozen up opposite Lyme,
or somewhere else in the Connecticut River,
and would not appear with its precious cargo
until the next spring.   Such were the difficulties of sending a box one hundred and ten
miles across Massachusetts in the year 1830.

To putting an end to such difficulties by
the railroad system, my father gave much of
the active part of his life, as I have before said.
When it was thought crazy to talk about such
things he talked about the possibilities of a
railroad westward.   When it was necessary to
induce men of capital to subscribe, with infinite difficulty he obtained a subscription of
a million dollars capital for the Boston and
Worcester Railroad.   He was the first president
and first superintendent of that railroad, and
had the great joy of importing its first engine
from Liverpool.   This, as I have said, was the

Meteor ; she was ordered from George Stephenson himself, immediately after the success of the *Rocket* in the famous railway trial between Liverpool and Manchester in 1830. The arrival of the *Meteor* in Boston, with the engine-driver who was to set her up and to run her first trips, was a matter of great joy to us boys. At the same time the *Yankee* was built by a company in Boston, at their works at the cross-dam of the Mill-dam ; and an engine always called the *Colonel Long* was built for the Boston and Worcester Railroad at Philadelphia, under the auspices of the same Colonel Long who gave the name to Long's Peak at the West. He was in the engineer service of the United States, and this engine was built to burn anthracite coal.

The *Meteor* was at once set up in Boston, and started on her experimental trips. It is easy to see how much this would interest the men who had looked forward to her success, and, equally, how much it would interest their sons. The engine-driver was good to my brother and me, and we had the great pleasure of making some of the earliest of her trips with him. I have spoken of the opening of the road to West Newton. I think they must still have there the sign which was put up on David's hotel, representing the engine and car of the period. It ought to be preserved in some historical collection there. Boston roused itself to the new interest, and every afternoon eight cars went out to Newton and back, that people might say they had ridden on the new railroad. Many a straw hat was burned through by the cinders which lighted upon it, and many notions were gained for the future.

What is now called the American system of the interior arrangement of cars, was first tried in the cars built for the Worcester Railroad at Worcester, by the founder of the present firm of Bradley. The suggestion was made, I believe, by my father; he saw very early the difficulty of the old system, in which the conductor ran around on a platform on the outside. I remember, as among the close approaches to death which in any man's life stand out distinctly, that, when I was in college, I ran after a train on which I was to go to Natick, sprang upon it when in

motion, and felt myself falling. I supposed
that the last instant of my life had come
while I fell for the first few inches. Then I
found myself astride of the long, narrow platform on which I had intended to stand.
Risks like this were what all the conductors
of the early railroads ran ; and I suppose,
indeed, the English guards may have to run
them, to a certain extent, to the present day.

The Boston and Worcester station in 1833,
and for some time after, was on the ground
now occupied by Indiana Street and by Brig-
ham's milk depot, between Washington Street
and Tremont Street. Tremont Street had just
been laid out on the level of the salt marshes.
It was at the instance of the Worcester Railroad that its grade was raised, many years
after, and that company was obliged to take
the cost of lifting the houses which had been
built on the lower level. It is to that change
of level that we owe it that the whole South
End of Boston is now built on the level above
the marsh, instead of being built, as the few
houses originally on it were, scarcely above
the level of high tide.

CHAPTER VIII.

THE WORLD BEYOND BOSTON.

ALL boys, from the nature of their make-up are great politicians. The boys of sixty years ago were not unlike boys of to-day in this matter, and, when an election day came around, we were glad to spend as much time as we could at the places where people were voting. Happy the boy to whom some vote distributor would give a handful of votes, and happier he who could persuade someone to take a ballot from those which he had given to him. This, by the way, was not very long after the time when a certain superstition held in Massachusetts by which every ballot was written. Early in the century gentlemen interested in an election would call on the women of the family, if they could write well, to write out ballots which could be used at the polls. But I never saw such written ballots.

The separation between Boston and the rest of the world affected a good deal the political combinations. I do not suppose that our present compact system of national political parties could possibly exist without the convenience of the telegraph and the railroad. I should say, historically, that it began in the great convention of young men which was held in the city of Baltimore in the year 1840 by way of advancing the election of President Harrison. Independent and sovereign as Massachusetts was in the election of 1836, her National Republicans, as they called themselves, nominated Mr. Webster as candidate for President, though nobody else nominated him, and the electoral votes of Massachusetts were given for him and for Mr. Granger. The leaders of any American party would hesitate before they should make such a separate demonstration now. And this habit of separation shows itself more distinctly in the newspapers of the time.

I have already said that I was a great deal in the printing-office of the *Daily Advertiser*, which my father edited, as well as in his book-office. He maintained with care and interest the old system of apprenticeship, and always had one or more bright boys, whom he had taken into his office that they might learn the whole art and mystery of printing and what concerned the publication of a newspaper. One of these young men, to whose counsels and help we boys were largely indebted, still lives, honored in the community where he has been known for many years, as the director of the Barnstable *Patriot*—Mr. Sylvanus Phinney. To have a boy a little older than yourself as your comrade in the office, to have him show you what you could handle and what you could not handle, was in itself a piece of education.

Mr. Phinney could perhaps tell better than I can, a newspaper story, not of my boyhood, but of girlhood in Boston. In the year 1820 the convention met which revised the constitution of Massachusetts. The *Advertiser* published the full report of the proceedings, and this report was made up in my father's workroom, in the lower story of the house in Tremont Street. He was suffering at that time from an accident by which he nearly lost the sight of one of his eyes, and all his writing was done at home by my mother. So it would happen of an evening that the gentlemen most interested in the convention would look in at the house to revise the reports of their own speeches, and perhaps to consult about the work of the next day. Mr. Webster and Judge Story were two of the prominent leaders of that convention. They were on terms of the closest intimacy at our house, and would come in almost every evening for this purpose. Mother would be sitting in the room to do any writing which might be required, and, lest she should be called away to the baby of the time, the baby lay asleep in the cradle while the work of dictation went on. Speeches were made, proofs corrected, baby rocked, and undoubtedly a great deal of the fun of such bright young people passed to and fro with every evening.

Afterwards, in friendly recognition of the hard night-work of the winter, when the convention was well over, and its proceedings were published in a volume which is now one of the cherished nuggets of the collectors, mother had a great cake made for the workmen at the office. She frosted it herself, and dressed it with what in those days they used to call "cockles" of sugar. These cockles generally had little scraps of poor verses, which were supposed to be entertaining. But in this case she had cut out from the proofs the epigrams of the convention debates, and as the apprentices and journeymen ate their cake they found, to their amusement, that the work of their own hands had furnished what were called the mottoes.

The journalist of to-day thinks he is much ahead of the journalist of that time, and in many regards he is ; but there were certain excitements which belonged to newspaper life then which do not belong to it now. The day when the *Unicorn* arrived in Boston, the first in the line of Cunard vessels which have arrived regularly from that day to this, was one of these exciting days. My father went over in person upon the *Unicorn*, talked with the officers, and came back with English newspapers almost as fresh as he had ever seen. I

say " almost as fresh," because the passage of
the *Unicorn* was, I think, twenty days, and we
had traditions in the office of rapid runs of
Baltimore clippers or other fast vessels which
had come over in less time. It was after this
that, in a winter passage, the *Great Western*
at New York brought news which was thirty-
five days later than the latest news which we
had from Europe. In earlier times there
would be many instances of longer periods
when neither continent knew anything of the
other.

Under such circumstances the newspaper
editor depended much more upon his foreign
correspondent than he does now. The foreign
correspondent of to-day digests news of which
he knows the details have already gone by
telegraph. He is in some sort a foreign editor,
but he does not expect to send the detail of
news. And there was an element of chance
about the arrival of sailing vessels which
added to the curiosity of your morning paper.
In our office Mr. Ballard, who had the charge
of the ship news, might board a vessel below
in the harbor, whose captain had no idea that

he had brought the latest news. Then this
poor captain would be beset to hunt up every
newspaper that he had on board. Perhaps
he had been so foolish that he had not bought
the last paper of the day on which he started.
Whether he had or had not it was the business of the boat which boarded him first to get
every paper he had, so that no other paper in
town might have a word of his intelligence.
Perhaps all these papers arrived at the office
but a little while before you went to press ;
then it was your business to make the best
show you could of the news, and possibly it
was your good fortune to be able to say that
no other paper had it.

I remember that we had the news of the
French Revolution of 1830, which threw
Charles X. from the throne, on a Sunday
morning. When such things happened the
foreman in the office made up what was really
an "Extra" by throwing together, as quickly
as he had them in type, a few galleys of the
news ; in that case probably rapidly translated from the French papers. Then these
galleys would be struck off on a separate

hand-bill, and such hand-bills were circulated as "Extras." And it is to this habit that the present absurd nomenclature is due by which one buys every day an "Extra" which is published at a certain definite time. All this is fixed upon my mind, because, when I came home from "meeting" on that particular Sunday, I was told the news that there was another revolution in France, and had the "Extra" given me to carry down to Summer Street, where one of my uncles lived. There is a certain picturesqueness about the receipt and delivery of news, when it comes in such out-of-the-way fashions, which the boy or girl of to-day finds it hard to understand.

Of course with type as much as we wanted, and all the other facilities for home printing, we printed our own newspapers. I do not think that at our house we did it so much as boys would to whom the making-up of a news-paper was not a matter of daily observation, involving a good deal of errand running and other work which was anything but play. But we older boys had the *Fly*, which was our newspaper, and my brother Charles, not long after, started the *Coon*, in the midst of the Harrison campaign, which survived for a good many years.

I believe that the last issue of the *Fly* is that which records the death of Lafayette, in 1836. We had not type enough then to print more than one page at a time. Three pages of the *Fly* had been printed, and the fourth was still to be set up when the news of Lafayette's death arrived. This was too good a paragraph to be lost, and we knew we could anticipate every other paper in Boston by inserting it. But unfortunately the *n*'s had given out. We had turned upside down all the *u*'s we had, till they too had given out. Also, still more unfortunately for printers in this difficulty, Lafayette had chosen to die of an "influenza," which disease was at that moment asserting itself under that name in France. It had not yet been called "la grippe," which would have saved us. We succeeded in announcing the death of "the good, generous, noble Lafayette," although "generous" needed one *n* and one *u*, and "noble" took one of the last *n*'s. The para-

graph went on to say that the death was
"caused by," and the last *u* was devoured by
"caused." Then came the word "influenza."
"The boldest held his breath for a time."
But we were obliged ignominiously to go to
press with the statement that his death was
"caused by a cold." This was safe, and
required no *n* and no *u*. Alas! in the making-up of the form the precious *n* of the word
"noble" fell out; and any library which
contains a file of the *Fly* will show that its
last statement to the world is that "the good,
generous, oble Lafayette has died; his death
being caused by a cold." Such are the exi-
gencies of boy printers in all times.

I have gone into detail as to the communica-
tions between the people in the country and
the people who lived in Boston, in the hope of
making the reader feel distinctly the isolation
which separated Boston from the rest of the
world. That isolation has left its marks on
the character of Boston till this day. It
explains the amusing cockneyisms of Boston
which make other people laugh at us, and a

certain arrogance of provincialism which crops out very oddly among people who have sons and daughters in every part of the world, and whose communication is now so free in every direction. " In the beginning it was not so." The people of Boston had a very large foreign trade from its origin till comparatively recent times. Now they have a little, and half their population is of a stock which came very recently from Europe. But in the beginning of this century there was very little immigration from Europe. Indeed, what there was was looked upon with a certain distrust. About the time I went to college, or a little later, a society of the most intelligent people in Boston was organized for the express purpose of keeping out foreign "immigration." We purists made a battle against that word. Professor Edward Channing would have resented the use of it in a college theme with the same bitterness with which Mr. Webster resented " in our midst"—a phrase which, I am sorry to say, you may now find almost everywhere. One of the most intelligent gentlemen in Boston was appointed to the business of keeping out immigrants—a business which can only be compared to Mrs. Partington's determination to sweep out the tide when it was rising in the English Channel! He had his office on Long Wharf, and wrote and forwarded circulars to Ireland to explain to the people of Ireland that they had better not come to this country. At the same moment the very people who paid his salary were building up a system of manufacturing and internal improvements which was actually impossible without the immigration which they had appointed him to check.

There was at that time, however, a distinct determination on the part of the best people in Boston that it should be absolutely a model city. They had Dr. Channing preaching the perfectibility of human nature ; they had Dr. Joseph Tuckerman determined that the gospel of Jesus Christ should work its miracles among all sorts and conditions of men ; they had a system of public education which they meant to press to its very best ; and they had all the money which was needed for anything good. These men subscribed their money

with the greatest promptness for any enterprise which promised the elevation of human
society.

In speaking of the lecture system I have
already stated their notion that if people only
knew what was right they would do what was
right.   So they founded first the Massachusetts Hospital, then its annex for the
insane ; then they made the State contribute
to the deaf and dumb asylum in Hartford ;
they established their asylum for the blind
at South Boston.   Indeed, they expected to
trample out every human ill, exactly as the
most optimistic young medical expert in New
York at the moment when I write these lines
expects to trample out every cholera bacillus
who shall present its little head in sight of
the lens of the most powerful microscope.
What these excellent people might have done
had Boston remained the funny little town it
was in the year 1820 I do not know.   But it
did not remain any such place.   The population was then 43,298 ; in 1830 it was 61,392.
The increase in ten years is forty-one per cent
of the population at the first enumeration—

an increase which would be thought very remarkable in the growth of any old city now. It indicates great prosperity. In the same ten years the population of the city of New York increased from 123,706 to 202,589, an increase of sixty-four per cent. Such figures should be remembered, by the way, by people who tell us that the present rate of the increase of cities is without precedent.

The growth, though rapid, and on the whole encouraging for the manufacturing system of New England, tended to divert capital to a certain extent from that foreign commerce which had been created and nourished by European wars. So soon as capital placed itself in one or another site of the interior, as Lowell, Manchester, Fall River, Holyoke, and the rest came into existence, so soon, of course, the Boston boy found out that there was a world outside of State Street and Milk Street. And now that Boston capital loves to place itself at any point where capital is needed, between Lockwood's Cape in 82° north latitude and Terra del Fuego on the outside of the Strait of Magellan, there is no longer an

opportunity for a Boston boyhood to be spent
in the conditions which surrounded me.
These were physically almost the same as
those which surrounded the boyhood of
Samuel Sewall in the seventeenth century, or
Henry Knox in the eighteenth.

CHAPTER IX.

AT COLLEGE.

I WAS but thirteen years and five months old when I entered Harvard College, so that these memories of a New England boyhood carry us into college life. For as early an entrance as this was not unusual in those days. My friend Dr. Andrew Preston Peabody entered college as sophomore in his thirteenth year—at the precise age of twelve years and six months; Edward Everett, twenty years before, entered at the age of thirteen. The first scholar of my own class, Samuel Eliot, afterward president of Trinity College, was but a few months older than I. I think we were the two youngest members of the class.

I have no idea that my father would have sent me to college so young but that my older brother was already there. We had always been together, and were absolutely attached to each other. In point of fact, at this moment, I should find it hard to think of any real knowledge of any sort which I have ever had, on any subject, of which I did not trace the "origins" to him. I suppose my father thought that he was the best adviser and instructor that I could have. Certainly he could not have sent me to Europe with any private tutor, with nearly the advantage which I received from being sent to Cambridge to live with my brother. Accordingly to Cambridge I was sent, although everybody knew that this was at a younger age than would be otherwise advisable. I should not certainly advise any one to send a boy to Cambridge at thirteen years of age now, though I believe there would be no difficulty in passing the Cambridge examinations at that age now, if a boy had been sensibly brought up, by teachers who understood what that examination is and is not. But the college was not then what it is now, and life after one left college was not quite what it is now. I have certainly never regretted that after I left college I had six clear years for seeing the world, before there was even an apparent necessity of my binding myself to the regular work of my profession. Now this could hardly have been had I entered college at the age of sixteen or seventeen, which was, I suppose, the age of most of my classmates.

It must have been on a morning in the end of August that this brother of mine and I started together, in my uncle's "chaise," which had been borrowed for the occasion, that I might present myself at six o'clock at University Hall for examination. The examinations are absurd enough now, but I think they do not make them begin at six in the morning. At that time, however, morning prayers were at six o'clock as soon as the term began, and it was considered proper that we should be introduced into the college routine at the beginning.

The examination was to last from six in the morning to seven in the evening on that day, and from six till two on the next day; and with the exception of an hour for dinner we were kept in the various recitation rooms all the time. After two on the second day we loafed round the yard, keeping near enough to the door of University Hall to know when we were called, one by one. Each person as he was called then entered what we afterwards called the "corporation room," where he found the president and members of the faculty, and each one received the announcement of his success or of his failure. You were admitted on probation, as it was called, there being a theory that you were not matriculated until the end of the first term. But we all knew that everybody who was admitted was matriculated ; and this was merely one of a set of traditional forms of which I will speak in another place.

I rather think that I derived a certain contempt which I have always felt for these mechanical functions called examinations from my experience on this occasion. As it happened, my brother and I arrived, in the chaise alluded to, early enough indeed, but later than the great body of the candidates, of whom there were about eighty. For instance, my own classmates of the Latin School had come out in an omnibus, which had been engaged to come at that early hour. We found, therefore, that they were already registered on the list of applicants, while my name came in at the very end, with certain other boys who had arrived separately. It is an illustration of the simplicity of those days that one of these boys at least had ridden twenty miles that morning, with his father, in the chaise in which they had come from Berwick in Maine. This was Francis Brown Hayes; his place in the alphabet brought him next to me in all the lists of our class, and we were intimate friends till the end of his life. Samuel Longfellow, who has lately died, was another of these sporadic persons; he had come with his father in a chaise from Portland in Maine, by a two days' journey.

We were told off into twelve sections, and proceeded to the examination. It was on much the same lines on which the examination is conducted now, with perhaps less of writing and more oral questions. There was, however, no examination in French or in German. I think the Latin and Greek and mathematics went as far as the required examination does now; but if a person wanted to enter in advance he presented himself on another day. In every class there were a great many persons in those days who "entered sophomore," as the phrase was. That is to say, the course was abridged to three years by these boys who had remained for two freshman years in the preparatory school. I believe that the persons most competent in the university are very glad to have some such course as this taken now; it is an easy way of solving the question whether the undergraduate course should be three years or four, and how much work should be thrown upon the preparatory schools.

I afterwards knew as teachers most of the gentlemen who conducted that examination. But there was one of them, who assigned us our places, gave us all general directions, and, in short, looked after us through the two days in the kindest manner possible, whom I did not meet again for many years. I now think it was Theodore Parker, whom I did not know personally till long after this time. I have ever since liked to think of him as showing such friendly sympathy and untiring consideration for the needs of seventy or eighty dazed and bewildered boys.

To us Latin School boys the examination was easy enough in most of its details. I know I went to it, and through it, with the light-hearted spirit in which it is best to meet life always, taking it for granted, that is, that I was at least equal to the average, and that, with good luck, I should come out better than the average. There was not one of us who had the slightest idea that he should not pass the examination. In fact, the only question I remember is the question whether Amsterdam were north of London ; this was put to a dozen or more of us, in a good-natured, friendly way, by George F. Simmons, afterwards an interesting and valuable preacher. Every one of the twelve answered the question wrong. We were not, however, conditioned on geography, although I do not remember that any other questions were put to me than this, on which I came out so badly.

When the examination was over it proved that but six of the eighty had passed "without conditions"; that was the phrase then, as I think it is now. Rather to the disgust and mortification of the five best scholars of our Latin School class, they were all conditioned. They were the five highest of the six Franklin Medal boys, and a Franklin medal is a type of the highest scholarship in a Boston school. Perkins, who was the sixth Franklin Medal boy, and I, who never had a Franklin medal, were the two from our school who passed without any conditions. I am disposed, as I say, to think that to this accident—for it was a mere accident—I owe the suspicion which I entertained as early as that period of my life that all these examinations are in a large measure humbugs. The persistence in them is one of the follies of our time, which will drop out, as various other follies drop out, from one generation after another. It seems to belong where patches on a lady's face belong, or similar customs, which one age thinks important and another age laughs at. Of course I went home very light-hearted, not to say proud; and from that day to this day I have never dreaded any of these formal functions, in whatever shape they have presented themselves. I am glad to think that my children have inherited something of the same light-hearted readiness to accept, without protest, any folly of the time, so it do not involve an essential principle.

But when the business of actually going to college began I had none of this light-hearted feeling. It was all very pleasant to go around with Fullum to furniture stores, with money enough to buy the chairs, and carpet, and washbowl, and other apparatus with which one was to begin independent life. It was interesting to go out with him to 22 Stoughton, and assist in putting the carpet down, in hanging the curtains, and in determining where my desk should be, and where my brother's should be, and so in beginning upon house-keeping. But when all this was over, when I had been to morning prayers for the first time, and had gone through the routine of morning recitations, and the first recitation of the afternoon —recitations which were all child's play to boys who had been as well trained as we— when I sat in the broad window seat, and looked out on the setting sun, behind Mount Auburn, as it happened, then the bitterness of the situation revealed itself to me. I was thoroughly and completely homesick.

I said to myself, perhaps I said aloud, "This is one day of three hundred and sixty-five, and that will make one year. At the end of that year I shall have gone through one of four such years." And I wondered how I ever could survive the deadly monotony of such a service. It was not till the next year that I read, in Miss Martineau's "Travels," that happy anecdote of the Jersey apprentice boy, who, when nine years old, was forever wishing for the Fourth of July. Some one asked him why he was so eager to have the Fourth of July come, and he said : "When that has come I shall have only eleven more years to serve." I repeat this tale of homesickness because, although it was an exaggerated feeling, it expresses well enough my dislike for the routine of college, a dislike which accompanied me to its very close. Other fellows took the thing more simply and philosophically. Newton, of my own class, a fine fellow who died young, said to me once that he attended every chapel exercise, morning and evening through the whole time he was in Cambridge. "Why should I not?" he said. "I had not the attractions which you had in Boston; Cambridge was my home. The rule was to be in chapel twice a day; I might as well be there as anywhere else." He was undoubtedly the happier and, I think, the better man, because he could accept the routine of life with such good nature.

As for the business which took us to college, more than half of us soon found out that we had been too well prepared. As Hayward used to say, "We had overrun the game." That is the great merit of the elective system, if it holds in the freshman year of a college— that a boy or young man can take hold where he is prepared to go forward. For us, however, we were set on reading Livy and Xenophon. These authors are easier after you have "the hang of it" than the Latin and Greek which we had been reading for some time before at school. We could almost read them at sight. Our teachers in these two

languages regarded the whole thing as a bore;
they were preparing for other fields in life,
and they had taken their tutorships by the
way, without any idea that they were to interest us in language or that there was much
interest in it; at least that is the impression
which they left upon our minds.   It was
simply a dull school exercise.   It may be said
in passing that one of the great difficulties
of our present college system comes from
the fact that in general boys, for the last year
they are in the preparatory school, have been
under the care of a gentleman of spirit,
and intelligence, and eagerness in education, who makes them his companions, who
gives them such enthusiasm as he has in the
studies which they are pursuing.   For then
they pass into the hand of some instructor
who has just graduated, who does not know
much, and very likely does not know how to
teach what he knows.   From a superior, picked
man, one of the best educators in the country,
perhaps, a boy passes under the direction of
a frightened novice, with whom the college is
trying an experiment whether he will or will

not succeed. Of course, in theory, the best educators ought to have the charge of those pupils who need education most. But in practice, I fancy, it is very hard, in the charge of colleges, to make the professors of most ability take those elementary duties upon themselves. Certainly in very few colleges do they take any such duty.

In the business of mathematics the whole thing was different. I find by the Quinquennial Catalogue that Professor Peirce, now well known as one of the most distinguished mathematicians of the century, was appointed two years before this time as Hollis Professor of Mathematics. He was but twenty-six years of age. It has been the custom to say that he was not a good teacher of mathematics, because his insight was so absolute that he made one long step where a pupil needed to make four or five, and that he could not understand the difficulty of the boy who did not see what he saw. I suppose this is true; but, on the other hand, he was an enthusiast in his business, he was sympathetic and kind where he saw real interest in the pupil, and he devised the best method for the handling of a class which I have ever seen. In his case, certainly, there was no right to complain that an inferior teacher was put in charge of novices. At two o'clock in the afternoon we went into one of the large dining-rooms of University Hall, which was not needed for commons. As one went into the room he took from a pile of manuscript books his own book, as he had left it the day before. In this book he found a slip of paper with the problem of geometry which he was to work out that day. Now if he had failed the day before the problem given him would be one on the lesson of the day before; if he had not failed it would take him on in the regular order.

Of course it happened, before many weeks were over, that the different members of the class were in different places ; but it also was sure, that nobody had been advanced any farther than he had understood what he was about. In point of fact, only six or eight members of the class went through without any failures at all, and the others straggled along in their places behind. If you had any real hitch, and did not understand the thing, you were encouraged in every way to sit down by Mr. Peirce and work out the problem with him.   We came to be, from that very moment forward, on terms of a certain sort of intimacy with him, which did not exist with five other teachers in college.   He was very cordial and sympathetic, if anybody used his own brains enough to work out the problem in a way different from that in the book ; and I doubt if I have ever received any honor in life which I prized more than the words "excellent and original," which once or twice he wrote at the bottom of my exercise.   Probably I hardly need say that this sort of intimacy led to a cordial friendship between him and me, which lasted till the very end of his distinguished life.

But there is a queer thing about this recitation with him, which shows the absolute indifference of the American world of the first half of this century to matters of physical health. When, in the year before, Francis Lieber was intrusted with the preparation of the fundamental rules for Girard College, he prepared a

curious code of such rules, in which he made
this his Article 227 :

No scientific instruction proper should be given
within a full hour after dinner. The contrary leads to
vice.

In utter indifference to any such rule as
this—probably in utter ignorance that there
was any connection between body and mind
worth notice—our whole class was ordered
into this mathematical exercise at two o'clock,
after we had dined at a dinner beginning at
one.   It was not till five years afterwards that
I stumbled on Lieber's axiom, which is based
on absolute experience ; and I think one may
doubt whether anybody at Cambridge cared
whether there were any such axiom or not.
Take, for another instance, the morning recitations.   We went into chapel at six, to a per-
functory service which lasted rather less than
ten minutes.   Half the class then went at once
into a recitation—whatever happened to be
convenient—although breakfast was not to be
served until twenty minutes past seven.   All
through the college year this same distance between breakfast and prayers prevailed ; what

was called the "half-hour bell" being rung half an hour after prayers were over, so that some sections went in then, as some sections had gone in immediately on the close of chapel. The absolute wickedness of working the brains of boys who had taken no food perhaps since five o'clock in the afternoon before, did not seem to occur to a human being in the administration.

My friend the late Dr. Muzzey, who was in college a dozen years before me, told me that, until he was a senior in college, nobody had ever told him that students ought to take physical exercise daily. He told me that he lived in the college yard, at work on his studies, day in and day out, without thinking that physical exercise was necessary for any reason, and that nobody told him that it was. It was not till he broke down, in a confirmed dyspepsia, from the results of which he suffered till the end of his days, that some physician explained to him that he ought to have taken some physical exercise every day of his life. It was true that Dr. John Ware, a person eminently fit for the duty, delivered lectures on the art of preserving health, to which we were obliged to go in our senior year. But the joke was that we did not go till our constitutions were destroyed.

Through the freshman and sophomore years it was impossible for any boy of more than average training and sense to spend more than three hours a day in preparing for recitations. Lectures, observe, were almost wholly unknown in those years. Then the college required three hours of recitation,—on some rare occasion possibly four. Here were six hours taken up by studies of the university. Supposing you slept nine hours out of the twenty-four (and I certainly did) here were nine hours to be got rid of in amusement of whatever kind, where we were absolutely our own masters. The requisition was simply that we should attend these recitations and chapel twice a day. In the summer half of the year chapel was at six in the morning, as I have said. As the sun began to rise later than six, the chapel was pushed forward so that the exercises might be carried on by daylight, for it had been proved, by sad experience, that the undergraduates took measures to put out the candles on which the chapel then depended for its light, if there were not light from the heavenly bodies. Given these requisitions, we might do as we chose for the rest of the time.

For many of us—certainly for me—a considerable part of this time was used in the library. The library then consisted of about fifty thousand volumes, which occupied the second story of Harvard Hall. With perhaps twenty exceptions every one of these books might be taken down by every comer and read, so only he remained in the library while reading. I think Mr. Emerson refers somewhere to the facility thus given and to the use of it, as the best advantage which a college has to offer. I remember that there was a proposal made once that he should reside in Cambridge, with a college appointment, as director of the reading of the undergraduates. Without any director or direction we browsed over the whole range of English literature, and, when we could, dipped into other languages. I wonder, when I look back on the miscellaneous reading of

those days, that even two or three hours a day
gave time for it.   But, practically, when you
had nothing else to do between ten and four,
you went into the library.   You sat at the
great table, where was Rees's Cyclopædia, and
you read the articles which you fancied or
needed.   You worked up your themes and
forensics there.   For me, I know I dipped
through the *Gentleman's Magazine*, from
1720 down.   I remember reading the folios of
adventure on the North-west coast, so that ten
years afterwards I was not unprepared for
Sutter, the Sacramento, the wreck of the
Peacock, and the discovery of gold.   It had,
in fact, been discovered by Shelvocke in 1718.

For home reading, that is, reading in our
rooms, we had the society libraries.   All this
has changed since you can buy a paper-cov-
ered novel for ten cents.   The society assess-
ments were not large—perhaps two dollars a
year.   For sixty members this gave an income
of one hundred and twenty dollars, to be spent
on the two-volume novel of the period, generally in Carey & Lea's Philadelphia reprint.
Cooper's later novels, James's novels, Mrs.

Trollope's, Mrs. Gore's, and plenty more, of which names and authors are now forgotten, were regularly bought and ready for distribution at our mutual circulating libraries. The first of Dickens's came in my time, and Bulwer still held the field. I and my brother were entitled to four such novels a week—eight volumes. I doubt if I averaged more than four volumes a week. But I am sure I read as many as that, and I think they did me much more good than hurt. The novelists of that day did their best in conversation, and for care in conversation I doubt if there is better training than the reading of good novels of that school. Of course we went back to the older books. Scott still reigned supreme. I knew Miss Austen by heart, almost, and we read everything else which the law of selection had preserved.

The necessity of these libraries—a necessity which no longer exists—kept the literary societies alive. The clubs, like the Hasty Pudding and the Porcellian, were a different thing; they had their libraries also.

The I. O. H. and the Institute were the

freshman and sophomore societies — the Union and the Hasty Pudding came later. There was the slightest possible pretence of rivalry between the societies of the Institute and the I. O. H., but it amounted to nothing. In practice each society met once a fortnight, and the Tuesdays of meetings alternated with each other. In each society the exercises began with a lecture, so called, which lasted five or ten minutes. You had to get up some subject, and make it as interesting as you could, and read it to the assembled thirty or forty fellows. Then there was a debate, to which two or three speakers were assigned on the affirmative, and two or three on the nega- tive. The fellows sat round the tables, which were built into the floor, for use when they should be needed in commons, and, after the regular speakers, anybody might join in the discussion. The discussions were of course as good and as bad as the discussions of boys generally are. But we were all trained by them to think on our feet, and all learned there to stand without our knees shaking under us, and that is the great thing to be learned. For the rest, if a man has anything to say he will be very apt to find out how to say it.

I am always sorry when I hear of any college that there is no interest in debating societies. Somehow or other you want to have Americans used to face an audience, and to tell the truth in as simple a way as it can be told ; and I know of no training so good for this as that of the debating club. I am glad to see that, under the auspices of the Lyceum League, there is a chance that the old-fashioned debating club may be revived.

Once or twice a year there was a more formal function in society life. You celebrated Washington's birthday, or something else which it was convenient to celebrate, by an oration and a poem. Then you invited the members of the other societies to come in.

The Davy Club had been in existence some years, under one and another name, before my day, and had the north-east corner room in the basement of Massachusetts for a laboratory. Dr. Webster, who was the professor of chemistry, gave us the most good-natured and

kindly assistance. Many a bit of old apparatus, for which substitutes had been found in
the college laboratory, was transferred for our
use ; and we might, at any moment, run over
to him for advice or information. We had
quite a little store of chemicals, and, on the
whole, the facilities of the Davy laboratory
were so much better than those which we
could concoct in our own wash basins and
what were called the "studies"—the little
closets by the sides of our chimney-places
—that we ordinarily stained our trousers and
our fingers in that laboratory rather than in
our own rooms.

In my senior year a dramatic event crossed
the deadly monotony of college life, which
sent a knot of us into the laboratory for the
whole of one Sunday. At morning chapel
President Quincy, with a good deal of
emotion, told us that breakfast at commons
must be delayed a little while on account of
an accident which had happened in the
kitchen. It proved that two of the waiters
had gone to sleep, in one of the rooms in the
basement which was assigned for their bed-

room, with a pan of charcoal burning. They had only been discovered just before chapel, and both of them were unconscious. At that moment the doctors were with them, hoping to re-arouse the vitality which was almost gone. When we came to breakfast a message came upstairs from this sick room, to know who there was at breakfast who could make oxygen. I ran down at once, and Dr. Wyman and Dr. Webster explained to me that they wanted to try the experiment of feeding the exhausted lungs with pure oxygen. When I found that it was not for immediate use only, but that the treatment was to be continued through the day, I told Dr. Webster that we should have to start the furnace in the Davy Club laboratory, and he bade me do so. With two or three others of the men most interested in chemistry I went up to that laboratory, and till ten o'clock in the evening we were sending down rubber bags of oxygen for these poor fellows to breathe. Whether it did them any good or not I do not know ; eventually one of them recovered and the other died.

I remember that our feet were wet through with the overflow of our pneumatic troughs; and, when we were notified that our work was needed no longer, I brought the whole crew up into my room in the third story of the same building to dry their feet and to take something warming within. We sat together for some time, and then they bade me good-night; but in two minutes one came rushing back for my water pails. It proved that the intense heat from our furnace, through the day, had cracked off the plaster in the chimney of old Massachusetts, and had exposed a timber which the careless builders of the year 1720 had only protected by rough-cast. Our fellows had prudently looked in at the laboratory as they went by, to see that all was safe, and had found themselves blinded with smoke. We went to work with a will to extinguish the fire we had lighted, but it was wholly shut in and was quite too much for us. That was the only night when I ever heard the traditional call of "Harvard." Some one ran out and called "Harvard, Harvard, Harvard!" two or three times lustily, and in two minutes we had all Harvard to help us. But all would not do. We had to call in the Cambridge fire department, to our great shame and grief; and it was not till, with their axes and pickaxes, they had cut away the chimney that we got at the beam to which we had set fire. Fortunately the old building was saved from destruction by the care of the men—Henry Parker is the one whom I remember—who looked in to see that all was safe after our day's work.

Another of these out of the way dabblings in science was our observations for meteors in the winter of 1838-39. This was organized by William Francis Channing, now so well known as the electrician. The New Haven astronomers had made the suggestion, which has since been generally accepted, that on the 12th of November annually the earth passes through a belt of meteors. Channing had had some conversation with Professor Lovering, who had told him that it was desirable that in November, 1838, there should be a careful observation on this subject; and we made a club of eight, which we called the Octagonal Club,

for the special purpose of making these observations. We sent a table and five chairs out
to the Delta. We met there in a squad at
midnight and after, and, back to back, sat, all
wrapped up, looking at the clear sky. We
were quite incredulous as to the "Novembre-
ity" of the shower ; we said that there would
be as many on any clear night ; and we under-
took to demonstrate it. So, month by month,
that winter, when there was no moon, we met
on the Delta in the same way to hunt for
meteors.

We have all been pleased since to see that
those observations are referred to in the careful studies of this business. We certainly
fixed the fact on the minds of the astronomers that on any fine winter night two or
three hundred meteors may be seen in our
clear sky, if there are enough people to look
for them. I doubt if this was generally
believed before the interest aroused by the
meteoric shower of November 12, 1833.

The recent observation, which seems to be
now generally accepted, that there are black
meteors, or moving bodies which reflect almost

no light to our world, has recalled to me these nights of observation. There were three or four of us who insisted upon it that now and then we saw black meteors. The others, of course, said this was merely the reaction of the retina, and all that. But it was one of the jokes which found expression in the little jingling poetry which among us we composed on those nights of observation :

> While Morison and Parker
> In south-east cry, " Marker,
> One jet black and darker
>   From zenith above";
> But Adams and Longfellow,
> Watching the throng below,
> Won't all night long allow
>   Black meteors move.

I think it was in the Natural History Society, however, that more of us were personally interested from day to day, than any other of these outside occupations. In imitation of the Davy Club we applied very early for one of the recitation rooms in the basement of Massachusetts, which the government cordially gave us, because they liked to help in such plans. Eventually we occupied all four of those rooms between the two entries. The whole basement is now given up to a large lecture room, the same which is used by the Phi Beta Kappa at its annual dinners. We were as poor as rats, and why we did not ask the college to furnish these rooms for us I am sure I do not know; I do not doubt they would have done it willingly. But we assessed ourselves terribly for the cases in which we were to keep our collections. And half my recollections of the Natural History Society are not of botany or mineralogy, but of bargains with carpenters and painters and other people who were to work for us in such details. I remember, on one occasion, we were very anxious to have the new rooms ready for a college exhibition, but two days beforehand the painters had not come. When they came I stood over them and made them promise that the paint should be dry by nine o'clock the next morning. They explained to me that if enough turpentine were used it would certainly be dry, and dry it was; but whether the fair friends whom we took to see our exhibition enjoyed the smell of the turpentine I have always since doubted.

And thus I am reminded that I have said nothing about college exhibitions. They have died out in the face of the pressure of modern life, I think from the difficulty that it was impossible to secure an audience. Probably the great festivity of class day takes the place of all such minor festivities. But in these prehistoric times of which I write the minor festivities held their own, and at the three exhibitions and at commencement there were large parties of ladies and gentlemen who visited the college, and who were entertained with more or less festivity. Exhibitions were divided into junior and senior exhibitions. This meant that the highest part in the junior exhibition was taken by the highest junior, while in the two senior exhibitions the highest parts were taken by the second and third seniors. This shall be explained more fully hereafter.

Now, as will appear, if you were in the upper twenty-four of the class you spoke twice before commencement came, and at commencement you had another part—oration, dissertation, disquisition, or a Latin or Greek part, according to your ability. So

much was matter of college regulation; but
the custom was that men who spoke invited
their friends out to hear them, and as there
were sixteen speakers at each exhibition, this
made a company of two or three hundred
ladies and gentlemen, who came out to "see
the colleges" on those particular days. On
those days there were no other college exercises; generally the Pierian was in attendance,
and they made pretty *fêtes* on a small scale, as
class day makes one of the grandest events of
the year now. If you had a part you rehearsed
for it, of course, with the teacher of elocution.
What was quite as important, you went down
to see Ma'am Hyde, who had a little shop on
Dunster Street, and you hired your silk gown.
You paid her fifty cents for a day's use of it.
She had enough of these gowns to answer for
the whole class, and unless a boy was the son
of a clergyman, or otherwise connected with a
good silk gown, he hired one of these for use.
They were very sleazy silk, and certainly
would not stand alone, but they answered the
purpose.

The exhibition itself began with a Latin

salutatory, in which you said civil things about the pretty girls, and thanked the professors and the president for their kindness to you. Then went on discussions of the character of Napoleon or of Alexander the Great, or speculations why there were or were not literary men in America, with a Latin or Greek dialogue translated backward from some modern poet. And after every four or five numbers there would be " music by the Pierian Sodality." While the music went on you walked around and talked with your pretty friends, or your uncles, or your aunts, and invited them to the spread at your own room; but the word " spread " was not then invented. So the sixteen numbers pulled through, every speaker bowing to the president and then to the audience, making his speech, bowing again, and retiring. There were certain "silent parts," as they were called, because the mathematical and chemical departments wanted to show who were their best men, irrespective of general college rank. These were assigned to three or four men, who wrote them out and tied them up in rolls with highly colored ribbon, and when their time came marched across the stage, made a bow to the presiding officer, gave the roll to him, made another bow to the president, and again retired.

This will be as good a place as any to tell the varying fortunes of class day itself, of which I happen to remember one of the most important crises. Class day seems to have originated as early as the beginning of the century. The class itself chose a favorite speaker as orator, and some one who could write a poem, and had its own exercises of farewell. There grew up side by side with those farewell exercises the custom by which the class treated the rest of the college, and eventually treated every loafer in Cambridge. As I remember the first class days which I ever saw, they were the occasions of the worst drunkenness I have ever known. The night before class day some of the seniors—I do not know but what all—went out to the lower part of the plot, where there was still a grove of trees, and "consecrated the grove," as the phrase was, which meant drank all the rum and other spirits that they liked. Then, on the afternoon of class day, around the old elm tree, sometimes called Rebellion Tree and sometimes Liberty Tree, which stood and stands behind Hollis, all the college assembled, and every other male loafer who chose to come where there was a free treat. Pails of punch, made from every spirit known to the Cambridge innkeepers, were there for everybody to drink. It was a horrid orgy from end to end, varied, perhaps, by dancing round the tree.

With such memories of class day President Quincy, in 1838, sent for my brother and one or two others of the class of that year in whom he had confidence, to ask what could be done to break up such orgies. He knew he could rely on the class for an improvement in the customs. They told him that if he would give them for the day the use of the Brigade Band, which was then the best band we had in Boston, and which they had engaged for the morning, they felt sure that they could change the *fête*. The conditions, observe, were a lovely July day, the presence in the morning at the chapel, to hear the addresses, of the nicest and prettiest

girls of Boston and neighborhood with their
mammas, and the chances of keeping them
there through the afternoon. Mr. Quincy
gladly procured the band, and when the day
came it became the birthday of the modern
"class day," the most charming of *fêtes*.
Word was given to the girls that they must
come to spend the day. In the chapel Cool-
idge delivered a farewell oration. Lowell,
alas! was at Concord, not permitted to come
to Cambridge to recite his poem; it had to be
printed instead. When the ode had been
sung the assembly moved up to that shaded
corner between Stoughton and Holworthy.
The band people stationed themselves in the
entry of Stoughton, between 21 and 24, with
the window open, and the "dancing on the
green," of which there are still traditions,
began. The wind instrument men said afterward that they never played for dancing
before, and that their throats were bone dry;
and I suppose there was no girl there who had
ever before danced to the music of a trombone.
When our class came along, in 1839, we had
the honor of introducing fiddles. I shall send

this paper to the charming lady—the belle of her time—with whom I danced in the silk gown in which I had been clad when I delivered the class poem of my year. Does she remember it as well as I do?

Commencement was a function far more important than the exhibitions or than class day, which, to speak profanely, were side shows. No audience can ever be persuaded to sit six hours or more to hear perhaps thirty addresses. So now, while a certain theory is maintained that certain of the best scholars in the large graduating class prepare addresses, by far the larger number of them are excused, and only five or six speakers, representing four or five branches of the university, actually address the audience. No one has to be in the theatre more than two hours.

But in the first half of the century the function consumed the day. People had more time, and, with a certain ebb and flow of the assembly of auditors, the First Church was kept full all day. Originally there was a recess in the middle of the day for dinner, I think, but of this I am not sure. In our day about twenty-five of the graduating class spoke, and there were one or two addresses by speakers who represented the " Masters," that is, those who took their second degree, three years after they graduated.

A " Master " might have fifteen minutes, I think. The three seniors who had " orations," that is, the highest scholars in the graduating class, had ten minutes. In order of rank there followed dissertations, disquisitions, and, if anybody could write verse, a poem. A dissertation was eight minutes long, and a disquisition four. Of all this you were notified when you were appointed.

My sophomore year began at the time when the high consulting powers had determined to celebrate the second centennial of the college. It was two hundred years since the granting of the charter, and that was, fairly enough, taken as the birthday.

Preparations were made to illuminate the buildings, and a great tent, in which two thousand people might dine, was pitched near where President Eliot's house now stands.

The president's house then was what we now call "Wadsworth," the house built for Benjamin Wadsworth by the province when he came from the First Church in Boston to be president of the college in 1726. Students would not be students if they did not connect some utter absurdity with every function; accordingly there was circulated among us a rumor, for which there was not the slightest foundation, that, in revenge for the burning of the Ursuline convent two years before, the Irish of Boston proposed to attack the college and destroy the illuminations the night before the celebration. To prepare for this attack the undergraduates met, and chose their officers for a night watch to protect the university. We took our turns as patrols all round the college yards, challenging every poor night wanderer who passed, and making him give the countersign. If he did not know it we bid him pass, and thanked God we were rid of a knave. It was, of course, an admirable preparation, worthy of our years, for a very fatiguing day of festival, thus to knock out three or four hours of sleep from the night before. The military company, called the Harvard Washington Corps,

"The hybrid band of Mercury and Mars,"

had been extinct for some years, but there lingered still, as "transmittenda," a few guns, sashes, and belts, with a sword or two, which served for the equipment of our officers. I doubt if there were a pound of powder among us all ; certainly not a bullet, flint, or percussion cap.

President Quincy delivered a historical address at this celebration which makes the opening chapter of his "History." I think it was on this occasion that the old motto "*Veritas*" was first drawn out from a manuscript record and used across the face of the three open books which are the bearing on the college seal.

At the dinner Mr. Webster, Mr. Everett, and Judge Shaw spoke, and I had, for the first time, the joy of hearing Wendell Holmes recite his own verses :

"Lord! how the seniors kicked about
That freshman class of one."

Perfect as they are to the reader, they are more than perfect when he stands on a bench at a college dinner and, with all his overflow of humor, of pathos, and of eloquence, recites them. Of how many Phi Beta dinners has he been the joy and crown! It is the first business of a Phi Beta president to make Dr. Holmes say he will come to the annual dinner, and the next is to catch any other celebrity who may have been a guest at commencement. Phi Beta is so free and easy that it is at that table that the brightest things are said. I remember to have heard there Lord Dufferin, Lord Ashburton, and Sir Edward Thornton among the travellers, and of our home orators Mr. Everett, Mr. Sumner, Mr. Hillard, Mr. Emerson, all the Quincys—yes, and so many more

All this gossip implies that we were kept alive and in motion for four years, but I have not told how the machine was fed and oiled. In earlier days every student ate his breakfast and supper in his room, taking "a size" from the buttery, and dining in commons. But we took all three meals in commons or at some private boarding-house.

University Hall had been built twenty-seven years before, for the general purpose of chapel, commons, and for providing reading-rooms. It was then supposed that one of the four large halls which crossed the building on the first floor would be used by each class in commons. But when I was in college only two halls were thus used; the two at the ends of the building, and the middle dining halls, as they were called, were reserved for large recitation rooms. It was in one of these that we recited to Mr. Peirce. As freshmen we all met for meals in the northern hall with the juniors. About half the undergraduates at that time lived in commons. Looking back on the fare which was served us I am rather surprised that they were able to do so much for us as they did, and do it so well. The bill of fare appears rather Spartan to young men of the habits of most of the young men who meet in Cambridge to-day. But the quality of our food was always good, and the quantity was such as would have satisfied a savage of the plains. I remember to have observed that I lost weight in vacations and gained weight during the months of term time.

The tables were firmly fixed into the floor, as if in memory of some time when, in rage, the guests had turned the tables up and flung them out of the window. We went to commons three times a day, the custom of men serving their own breakfasts and suppers in their own rooms having been given up not many years before. The buttery, as it was called, used to be at the east end of Harvard Hall, where a slight trace of the roof of that temporary building may, I think, still be seen; but in our days there was no buttery, and it was not necessary for any person to cook in his room. Everything which we really needed was provided for us at commons.

Eighty minutes after the morning prayer bell stopped we were rung in to breakfast. The breakfast was coffee or milk *ad libitum*, hot and cold bread, and butter. I think no meat was served at breakfast. We knew what would be the variety of the hot bread; it was made in different rolls or biscuits for different days, and the order was never changed. Dinner was at one, and always consisted of one sort of meat, potatoes, and something called pudding. Here, again, the bill of fare was as absolute as if it had been laid down by the Medes and Persians, and never changed. I think it is burned in on my memory so that, to this day, when certain provisions appear on certain days of the week, I take it as something preordained. For meats, Sunday was roast beef, Monday was corned beef, Tuesday was roast veal, Wednesday was beefsteak, Thursday was roast lamb or mutton, Friday meat-pie with fish, Saturday was salt fish. I think we never had pork in any form, either fresh or in the shape of ham. To make the Friday dinner more substantial meat-pie was added ; I suppose a house-keeper would tell us that it was made out of such meat as had not been eaten in the preceding days. We remember it because after eating this solid meat-pie we went to our rooms to write our Friday themes. The puddings were boiled rice, baked rice, hasty pudding, baked Indian pudding, apple pudding, and, on one day,

some sort of pie took the place of pudding.
Every now and then there would be a com-
plaint that the butter was bad ; in that case
we did not stand it. Somebody went right
round to the president and told him, and he
sent for the contractor and gave him a blow-
ing up. We always pretended at home and
elsewhere that the fare was not good, but it
was good.

Now the wonder to me is that they man-
aged to feed a set of ravenous wolves—for that
is what we were—on such a bill of fare, at the
prices at which food was then sold in Eastern
Massachusetts. Flour ranged in those years
from $4.90 a barrel to $11.50. But we paid
only $1.90 a week for our board in the first
year when I was in college, and $2.25, for every
year afterwards. It must be remembered that
this charge involved for the contractor no
expenses for crockery, silver, knives and forks,
rent, or fuel. The college had these to see to.

The table at which I sat became, in fact, a
club table ; we were the same little company
from the beginning to the end of our college
life. While we were in college Dickens's

books began to appear, and we made it a rule
that the table should buy the serial parts for
its own use ; one man bought the first number,
the next man the second, and we passed them
round.   We introduced into commons the
institution of salt-spoons.   Up to our time
every man put his knife into the salt-cellar;
but we subscribed twenty-five cents and bought
two salt-spoons made of bone, which we used
through our college course.   It was agreed
that they should be given to the man who was
first married.   Six years after, our excellent
friend Watson of Plymouth was married,
and we sent him the salt-spoons, set in silver
in a careful design made by Richard Green-
ough, who was the friend of all of us.   Longfellow and I were intrusted with the business
of mounting the salt-spoons, and we did so.
The inscription was from Lucian, suggested by
Longfellow : "῾Αλῶν ἐκοινωνοῦμεν" — " We
have shared each other's salt."

It is a little unsentimental, perhaps, to have
spent so much space on the physical business
of feeding the engines.   Still it must be confessed that in all human life armies have to be

fed, and even the future poets, philosophers, statesmen, and men of affairs of a country have to be fed for the same reasons. In point of fact, we were a healthy and a happy race. I have said, I believe, almost nothing about our athletic amusements; but there were enough of them, although they were conducted with utter lack of system, and would bring scorn, I suppose, on any one of us, or any eleven, who should reproduce them to-day. We had foot-ball in tumultuous throngs; we had base-ball, in utter ignorance that there were ever to be written rules for base-ball, or organized clubs for playing it; and we had cricket, in a way. So we wrought through the four years, which for me were, as I have said, tedious, as I had expected they would be. But every one of us made friends to whom he has clung through life, and we got an outlook into a larger world, even if we did not look into the largest. The jest with regard to Cambridge is that nobody who lives in Cambridge knows anything five miles from the sound of the college bell. This is not true now, and it was not any more true then; we acquainted ourselves with friends from all parts of the United States; we got broader views of politics and society than those we had picked upat home ; and we left college certainly willing to do our duty.

The great functions of college life which attract the outside world are now in the hands of the students.   They are the boat races, or the ball matches, or the other athletic "events"; or they are, perhaps, the theatrical performances of the Hasty Pudding, the concerts of the glee clubs, or the great annual festival of class day.   In our time this was hardly so ; when strangers came to college they came at the invitation of the government. There were three annual exhibitions, and commencement day was still the great festival of all.   The exhibitions were arranged with perfect deference to precedent and with absolutely mathematical care, so that you might know what was the precise grade of scholarship to which each student had attained; if he only belonged to the "upper half" of the class. "Upper half" was not a strictly accurate expression, but was sufficiently so to include the twenty-four men who had had the highest

rank on the numerical scale to which everything bent. In this scale every person was
marked for every recitation. If you made a
perfect recitation your mark was 8; if you
"deaded," as the phrase was—that is, if you
failed absolutely—the mark was 0; and the
mark took any figure between, according as the
teacher thought you were well prepared. For
certain exercises the mark was higher; for instance, a perfect theme, such as Longfellow used
to write, was marked 48, and a theme might
bear any mark below. Of these marks a great
total was kept. If you were absent from any
recitation, eight was deducted from your total.
If you were absent from chapel I think two
was deducted; every offence and every success
had its correlative weight on this absolute
standard.

I used to say, and it was perfectly true, that
if a man entered college absolutely well fitted,
so that at his first recitation he received 8 for
every exercise, and from that moment declined
in morals, in scholarship, and in intelligence,
so that at his last recitation he received 0 for
everything, his rank on the college scale the

day he graduated would be absolutely the same as that of some unfortunate who, having got into the college by mistake, received 0 for every mark on his first recitation, and then by assiduous study, virtue, and intelligence rose so that at the end of his course he received the highest mark for everything, and was the best scholar in his class. This statement was absolutely correct. The rank list, so called, of all colleges simply gives a miserable average of what a person has been in a certain period of time, and does not reveal, to men or to angels, anything of his present capacity or his present wish and intention.

By such a rank list, however, we were all measured. I think the result was a very great indifference to college rank on the part of most of the students. But in the bosoms of our families there was a great respect for it; everybody knew who the first scholar was, and there were traditions of the first scholars of a hundred years before us, so that a certain interest attached to knowing who the first scholar was. This interest was met in our case, and it would have been in the case of all other classes of our

time, when what was called the sophomore
exhibition, which has been already alluded to,
came on. With us it was at the end of the
college year of 1836–37. On a certain morning
in May eight of our fellows were sent for to
go to the president. They had little slips of
paper given them, telling them what parts were
assigned them for the exhibition, which was to
take place just before the end of the college
year. These parts were translations into Latin
and Greek, or from Latin and Greek into English ; but these eight then knew that they were
the eight highest scholars in our class. For
the same exhibition one English oration was
assigned, with which the exhibition closed.
The junior who received this part knew that
he was the highest scholar in his class then ;
unless he failed badly in the next year this
man would be sure to receive the highest honor
at commencement.

There were, as I have said, three of these
exhibitions in a year, and at each exhibition
eight of one class and eight of another were
appointed, making sixteen in all. The exhibition consisted of declaiming these parts, of

which the half were translations and half were original, in English, Latin, or Greek, before such an audience as chose to come together. Most of the students were at that time from the eastern part of Massachusetts; it would therefore happen that sixteen students might call together two or three hundred of their friends to hear their performances on such occasions. You spoke, in a black silk gown, for four minutes, for six minutes, for eight minutes, or for twelve, according to your rank; you delivered a poem, or a disquisition, or a dissertation, or an oration, or you had your part in a "forensic," or perhaps simply declaimed in a dialogue which you had translated from some English drama into Greek or Latin. After the exhibition you asked your friends to your room, where there was a modest entertainment provided; the word "spread" is now used for such entertainments, but that has come in since my time.

At the end of the whole business, when your boyhood was all but over, and your manhood was about to begin, the college commencement ended the whole. Still it was rightly enough named, for it was the beginning of life. To prepare for this the president's freshman carried round, not sixteen notes, but twenty-four or more, to call to the president's study the seniors who were highest in rank of the class which was to graduate. They were to receive their bachelor's degree. You went round to the president, and he gave you a slip of paper :

"Jones, a disquisition, four minutes";

or,

"Smith, an English dissertation, eight minutes";

or,

"Brown, an English oration, twelve minutes."

Then you had the summer term to get up this part. You carried it down to Mr. Channing, who struck out its exuberant rhetoric, you rehearsed it to the teacher of elocution, you hired your black silk gown of Mrs. Hyde, and all was ready. The morning of commencement, before daylight, there began a queer procession from Boston of people, who were generally black people, with little covered handcarts or other vehicles, with which they established

themselves around the Cambridge Common to
feed the thirst and the hunger of the loafers of
that town. With them and theirs, however,
students had little or nothing to do. But, for
the multitude of Cambridge, commencement
was thus made much more a public holiday
than was any other day in the year.

At eight o'clock in the morning the Governor
rode out from the State House in a barouche
with an escort of cavalry; the officers and
the corporation rendered themselves; and at
the First Church, which had been fitted up
with a platform, the exercises began at nine
o'clock. Lucky was the class and lucky were
the spectators if they were done at half-past
three in the afternoon. Perhaps one or two
speakers had been added to the twenty-four
who had had parts at exhibitions. It was generally considered that, out of respect to the
nine Muses, if you had a poet of marked excel-
lence in the class, he had a part whether he
had or had not earned it by being one of the
first twenty-four. Some fellow who wrote
Latin decently well made a Latin salutatory.
He said something funny about the girls, he

complimented the professors, and told the
governor that all men considered themselves
fortunate that the Commonwealth of Massachusetts was under his direction. Then in
stages of four or five parts at a time you went
forward and satisfied yourself whether Alexander the Great were or were not a robber,
whether literature would or would not flourish
in America, and whether Julius Cæsar or
Napoleon were the greater general. For
glimpses of relief, as these numbers flowed on,
the band performed some music, and people
who could not stand it any longer then got up
and went out, and people who had been waiting outside came in. So the exercises flowed
on in a steady stream till, as I say, between
three and four o'clock, when the president
was ready to give the degrees. He gave the
bachelor's degree to these youngsters who had
been speaking the pieces and to the rest of the
class. The classes, on an average, were about
sixty at that time. Then he called up those
who were to be admitted as Masters. This was
simply a file of such of the graduates of
three years before as chose to pay the fee for

another diploma. All the same, they were represented in the speaking by some one who delivered what was known as "the Master's oration." It was rather longer than the other orations, and was supposed to be more manly.

I may say in passing that I think the only tribute to college rank which I have ever known conferred by this active world of America was in connection with one of these Masters' orations. A man whom I knew rather well when I was in college had the Master's oration of his year. Ten years afterwards, as it happened, he was in a distant city, where, he told me, he had gone to see the lady whom he was afterwards to marry. Rather to his surprise, he found himself quartered in his hotel in what was known as the "Governor's room," a handsome parlor on the first floor, with all the conveniences of bedroom on one side, a bathroom, and the rest, such as in those days were not often dispensed in a travellers' hotel. When he paid his bill he asked to what accident he owed this distinction. And the "gentlemanly clerk" at the office said: "I heard you speak your Master's oration at Cambridge ten years ago." So it seems that feudal institutions did linger in America almost as late as the middle of this century, and that the men of the carnal world had still some honors to confer on those who had in any sort been favored by the Muses.

And with this distribution of degrees college life ended. The degree is in Latin, and it does not promise much. It does give you the privilege of speaking in public whenever anybody asks you to. This privilege is one apt to be claimed by the American boy or the American man when he has not studied in a university. That is to say, any man may "hire a hall." There is, perhaps, a satisfaction in being authorized to do so in a language which few people understand, by a body of men who have received from the commonwealth the right to give such authority. However that may be, it is quite true that at the moment when one receives a piece of parchment which gives him this privilege his boyhood may be said to end and his manhood to begin.

THE END.

EAST AND WEST.

A Story of New-born Ohio.

By EDWARD EVERETT HALE,

AUTHOR OF "THE MAN WITHOUT A COUNTRY," "TEN TIMES ONE ARE TEN," "IN HIS NAME," "SYBIL KNOX," ETC.

1 Vol., 12mo, Extra Cloth, $1.00.

FOR SALE BY ALL BOOKSELLERS.

CASSELL PUBLISHING COMPANY,

104 AND 106 FOURTH AVENUE, NEW YORK.

A NEW MINE OF DELIGHT FOR YOUNG FOLKS

WILL BE FOUND IN

FAIRY TALES IN OTHER LANDS.

By JULIA GODDARD.

1 Vol., 16mo, Cloth, with 86 Illustrations, $1.25.

" Entertaining stories, charmingly told."—*St. Paul Pioneer Press.*

" Related with a rare and simple grace . . . a valuable contribution to comparative folk-lore."—*New Orleans Picayune.*

" A very fascinating work."—*Boston Home Journal.*

" A pleasant series."—*New York Times.*

" Will be welcomed by young people."—*Episcopal Recorder.*

" All good."—*Kansas City Journal.*

" Will serve to entertain many a family circle."—*Boston Courier.*

"Calculated to afford intense delight to little ones."—*New Haven News.*

" All children fond of reading will be charmed by these well written tales."—*Hartford Times.*

" Will be a source of perpetual delight."—*Ohio State Journal.*

THE CHARMING AND POPULAR
WORKS OF MRS. L. T. MEADE.

Very few authors have achieved a popularity equal to that of Mrs. MEADE as a writer of stories for young people. Her characters are living beings of flesh and blood, not lay figures of conventional type. Into the trials, crosses, in short, the everyday experiences of these the reader enters at once with zest and hearty sympathy. While Mrs. MEADE always writes with a high moral purpose, her lessons of love, purity, and nobility of character are rather inculcated by example than intruded as sermons.

BASHFUL FIFTEEN. 1 vol., 12mo, extra cloth, with eight illustrations, $1.50.

A SWEET GIRL GRADUATE. 1 vol., 12mo, extra cloth, with illustrations, $1.50.

A WORLD OF GIRLS. Illustrated. 1 vol., 12mo, extra cloth, gold and colored inks, $1.50.

POLLY: A NEW-FASHIONED GIRL. With full-page illustrations. 1 vol., 12mo, cloth, gilt, $1.50.

THE PALACE BEAUTIFUL. A Story for Girls. With eight full-page plates. 1 vol., 12mo, cloth, $1.50.

THE CHILDREN OF WILTON CHASE. 1 vol., 12mo, extra cloth, with illustrations, $1.50.

FOUR ON AN ISLAND. A Book for the Little Folks. 1 vol., 12mo, extra cloth, with illustrations, $1.50.

A RING OF RUBIES. 1 vol., 12mo, extra cloth, with illustrations, $1.50.

OUT OF THE FASHION. 1 vol., 12mo, extra cloth, with illustrations, $1.00.

CASSELL PUBLISHING COMPANY,
104 & 106 FOURTH AVE., NEW YORK.

FAMOUS BOOKS BY JULES VERNE.

MISTRESS BRANICAN.

By JULES VERNE.

Translated from the French by A. ESTOCLET. Illustrated by
L. BENETT.

**1 vol., 12mo, extra cloth, $1.00 ; paper, Cassell's Sunshine
Series, 50 cents.**

"Will rank among the author's best."—*New Haven Journal and Courier.*

"Teems with wonders and adventures which could only have found their birth
in the most imaginative brain of any living author."—*New York Observer.*

"Packed full with marvelous adventures hair-breadth escapes and strange
things seen in out-of-the-way places thousands of miles apart."—*San Francisco
Chronicle.*

"Jules Verne's admirers will welcome this addition to his narratives of adventure."—*Philadelphia Inquirer.*

"Intensely interesting. . . . Beneath the surface of all the writings of this
noted author there is an abundance of information which is sci ntifically accurate."
Iowa School Journal.

CÆSAR CASCABEL.

By JULES VERNE.

Translated from the French by A. ESTOCLET.   With all the original
French illustrations by GEORGE ROUX.

**1 vol., 12mo, extra cloth, $1.00 ; paper, Cassell's Sunshine
Series, 50 cents.**

*This book appeals strongly to American readers, the scene of more than
half of the story being laid in America.*

"The tale is one of the most thrilling and ingenious of Verne's writings."—
Boston Daily Advertiser.

"An extremely well told and entertaining story."—*New York Times.*

"A most characteristic and active romance."—*Christian Advocate.*

"Narrated with . . . inimitable story-telling art."—*Brooklyn Times.*

"Will be welcomed with delight by that large army of young readers for whom
he has written so much and so well."—*Boston Saturday Evening Gazette.*

"It is a book for old and young."—*American Bookseller.*

CASSELL PUBLISHING COMPANY,

104 & 106 FOURTH AVENUE, NEW YORK.